DANIEL WEBSTER.

Wit and Humor of the American Bar

A COLLECTION FROM VARIOUS SOURCES CLASSIFIED UNDER APPROPRIATE SUBJECT HEADINGS

THE LAWBOOK EXCHANGE, LTD.
Clark, New Jersey
2004

ISBN-13: 978-1-58477-387-0
ISBN-10: 1-58477-387-1

Second printing 2006

Printed in the United States of America on acid-free paper

THE LAWBOOK EXCHANGE, LTD.
33 Terminal Avenue
Clark, New Jersey 07066-1321

Please see our website for a selection of our other publications and fine facsimile reprints of classic works of legal history:
www.lawbookexchange.com

Library of Congress Cataloging-in-Publication Data

Wit and humor of the American bar: a collection from various sources classified under appropriate subject headings.
p. cm.
Originally published: Philadelphia: G.W. Jacobs, c1905.
ISBN 1-58477-387-1 (cloth: acid-free paper)
1. Law--United States--Humor. 2. Law--United States-Anecdotes.
I. Reddall, Henry Frederic, 1856-1921.

PN6231.L4W58 2003
818'.520208355--dc21

2003056441

Wit and Humor of the American Bar

A COLLECTION FROM VARIOUS SOURCES
CLASSIFIED UNDER
APPROPRIATE SUBJECT HEADINGS

PHILADELPHIA
GEORGE W. JACOBS & CO.
PUBLISHERS

Contents

Wit and Humor of the American Bar

CHAPTER I

Some Neat Replies

Legal Sarcasm

John R. G—— was in his day one of the most distinguished lawyers in New Orleans. Though not as learned as some of his associates at the bar, he possessed qualities of mind which rendered him a formidable antagonist. His personal appearance was much in his favor, and the gravity of his manner and his perfect self-possession contributed a great deal toward his standing as an advocate. His chief characteristic was audacity, which never failed him in any emergency. He was also a lawyer of very fertile resources, and if engaged in arguing a very weak case, he was not above resorting to trick or artifice to accomplish his purpose, which the following anecdote will illustrate:

In a case of appeal before the Supreme Court

he pretended to quote from time to time from certain authorities, and was for a while permitted to do so without interruption, the bar being accustomed to such breaches of professional propriety on his part. But on this occasion a recently appointed judge was on the bench, and when Mr. G—— spoke of a particular law he asked where it could be found. The old judges present smiled when they heard the question, for they were familiar with the ruses practiced by Mr. G——, but that gentleman, not at all disconcerted, responded that he thought it was in Story, giving volume, page, etc.

The imperturbable lawyer proceeded with his appeal, and in the interim a copy of Story was procured by the doubting judge, who was soon in earnest search of the authority in question. Failing, of course, to find it, he took advantage of the first pause in the speech of Mr. G—— to tell that gentleman he had been unable to meet with the law quoted. Whereupon Mr. G—— exclaimed:

"Is that so, your honor? Have I made so great a mistake?"

"You have indeed," said the judge. "Neither I nor my associates have ever heard of a law like it."

"Well, may it please the court," remarked

Mr. G——, very coolly, "if there is no such law in the books, *there ought to be!* for it would be founded alike in equity and common sense, which do not always govern the rulings of our courts of justice."

And he concluded his argument as if nothing unusual had occurred. The sarcasm with which he sought to cover up his exposure was not lost on those to whom it was addressed, but the incident which elicited it was related to his detriment for many years afterward.

He Probably Was

It was out West, in one of those local courts where a friendly talkative way marks the intercourse between judges, juries, counsel and clients. A man of the law, after developing considerable eloquence in behalf of a prisoner, perorated by saying: "Gentlemen, after what I have stated to you, is this man guilty? *Can* he be guilty? *Is* he guilty?"

Greatly to his disgust, the foreman of the jury replied: "You just wait a little, old hoss, and we'll tell you."

On the Best Authority

A story is told of a trial for burglary in which one of the jurymen seemed to be so certain of the prisoner's innocence, and pleaded for him so eloquently and so convincingly, that the eleven others (who had no particular leaning either way) allowed themselves to be argued into returning a verdict of "not guilty." A few days later fresh facts came to light, which proved the accused man's innocence beyond a doubt; and one of the eleven wavering jurymen, happening to meet with the man who had so powerfully influenced them all, thanked him warmly for having saved them from the commission of a great injustice.

"And yet, now I think of it," he added, "you could not have known *then* anything about these new facts, so how could you be so sure that the man was innocent?"

"Well," replied the other, "my chief reason for thinking that he did not commit the crime was that *I committed it myself*."

Where He Crossed the Equator

As one of the very few occasions when the wit of Rufus Choate was foiled, an incident is recalled when that brilliant lawyer was examining one, Dick Barton, chief mate of the ship *Challenge*. Choate had cross-examined him for over an hour, hurling questions with the speed of a rapid-fire gun.

"Was there a moon that night?"

"Yes, sir."

"Did you see it?"

"No, sir."

"Then how did you know there was a moon?"

"The 'Nautical Almanac' said so, and I'll believe that sooner than any lawyer in the world."

"Be civil, sir. And now tell me in what latitude and longitude you crossed the equator."

"Ah, you are joking."

"No, sir, I'm in earnest and I desire an answer."

"That's more than I can give."

"Indeed. You a chief mate and unable to answer so simple a question?"

"Yes, the simplest question I ever was asked. I thought even a fool of a lawyer knew there's no latitude at the equator."

Inspired Decisions

The father of William Jennings Bryan was a worthy citizen and an honest judge of the inferior bench of Illinois, who used always to open his court with a prayer for divine guidance in his rulings through the coming day. These rulings, though rendered in full faith that they were inspired, were nevertheless reversed again and again in decisions of the Supreme Court on appeal. When his attention was called to that circumstance, he waved the base inference aside with the declaration: "Well, I know that the Supreme Court is wrong and God is right!" And nothing could move him to any other view.

Time and Eternity

"I trust I am not unduly trespassing on the time of this court," once said a prosy counselor to a well-known judge.

"There is some difference," the judge quietly observed, "between trespassing on time and encroaching on eternity."

A Significant Silence

The Hon. Hilary A. Herbert, for a long time Congressman from Alabama and sometime Secretary of the Navy under Cleveland, has resumed the practice of law in Washington.

To his intimate knowledge of men and affairs during his terms of office may be ascribed the pith of the following anecdote:

Not long ago Mr. Herbert had occasion to call upon a certain official of the Treasury Department whose softly-modulated voice has gained him the designation of "the silent one."

The messenger to this official stopped the lawyer as he was going into the room, saying that his chief was "not in."

"Oh, yes, he is," said Herbert; "he's in there!" and he pointed to the room, the inside of which was not visible from where he stood.

"But, sir—but," began the puzzled and bewildered messenger, "how do you know that?"

"Because," chuckled Mr. Herbert, "it's so confoundedly still in there!"

Unprepared

The would-be advocate should have something to say, and yet a day spent in visiting our courts will suffice to show the astounding number of attorneys who rush before judges and juries with only superficial knowledge of the cases which they are supposed to try. Some sophist once "took a day off" and coined the phrase, "inspiration of the moment." There never was a more fallacious expression. Even Cicero's art failed him when he arose to defend Milo, leaning almost entirely on this slender reed. Frightened at the mob's cry for vengeance upon the murderer of the demagogue Clodius, the great orator stuttered a few sentences and was silent. Small good did it do the defendant that

Cicero afterward prepared the model of forensic display which is known to students as the "*Oratio pro Milone*," and forwarded it to his banished client, only to receive a half humorous, half sarcastic letter of thanks for its previous non-delivery. "For, had you spoken as you wrote," his friend observed, "I should doubtless not now be eating these excellent mullets of Marseilles."

He Did Not Die

In Brooklyn the attempt was made to discontinue a case on the ground that the plaintiff was dead. Whereupon his counsel submitted the following affidavit:

I did not die on December 23d, nor at any other time, but am alive and as well as I could be expected to be in view of the injuries inflicted upon me by the defendants. I do not wonder that they have moved to discontinue this suit on account of my death, as they had every reason to believe that the injuries inflicted on me had caused my death.

J. T. Hanning.

How John Sherman Became a Lawyer

General Jack Casement, the veteran railroad builder, who fought during the Civil War with General Sherman, and who was his intimate friend until the latter's death, tells the story of John Sherman's entrance into the practice of the law, as related by his warrior brother.

When John Sherman was quite young he was taken into the law office of his brother Charles at Mansfield, Ohio, to help about the office and make himself generally useful. One day, when he was in his twenty-first year, he took Charles to one side and quietly asked him for a loan of fifty dollars.

"What!" Charles exclaimed. "What do you intend doing with so much money?"

"I am going to Columbus to be admitted to the bar," John replied.

Charles was greatly surprised, as John had never asked him for any advice regarding the profession nor had he ever appeared to be interested to any extent in the study of law.

"You can't be admitted to the bar without some knowledge of the law," said Charles.

John maintained that he knew more about law than some others, and assured his brother that he would try to raise the money somewhere.

"You know," he added, "it will be necessary for me to have respectable clothes and enough money to pay my traveling and hotel expenses."

Charles finally ordered the clothes and provided him with the necessary money. At Columbus, on the day he became of age, John was admitted to the bar. On his return he said to Charles:

"I am going to Iowa to practice law."

Charles remonstrated with him.

"There is room for both of us to practice law here in Mansfield," Charles told him.

They then and there became partners and continued to practice together until the formation of the Republican party, when John was sent from the Mansfield district as a Representative in Congress.

CHAPTER II

The Bright Witness

A Star Witness

LAWYER EDWIN O. LEWIS, of Philadelphia, says that he recently came across the brightest witness that ever faced cross-questioning.

"It was a murder case," said Mr. Lewis, recounting the incident, "and my witness was on the stand. He had been in the vicinity of the spot where the crime was committed, and, naturally, was the star witness of the trial.

"'Will you tell the court how far you were from the spot where Mr. Blank was shot?' asked the counsel of the opposition.

"'I was just fourteen feet, eleven inches away,' replied the witness.

"'Will you tell me how it came about that you know the distance so specifically?'

"'I measured it, sir. I was pretty sure some fool would ask the question sooner or later.'

"Even the court gavel couldn't suppress the disturbance that followed this unexpected answer," finished Mr. Lewis, relighting his cigar.

"Yes" or "No"

It is not always easy to answer a legal question by a simple affirmative or negative. A browbeating lawyer once demanded that a witness answer a certain query by "Yes" or "No."

"I cannot do it," said the man on the stand. "There are some questions that cannot be so answered."

"Give the court an example!" demanded the lawyer truculently.

The retort came quick as a flash of lightning:

"Are you still beating your wife?" and the man of law, with a sickly grin, sat down.

Direct Evidence

The lawyer shook his finger warningly at the witness and said:

"Now, we want to hear just what you know, not what some one else knows, or what you think, or anything of that kind,—but what you *know*. Do you understand?"

"Wal, *I know*," responded the witness with emphasis, as he lifted one limber leg and laid it across the other. "I *know* that Clay Grubb said that Bill Thompson told him that he heard

John Thomas's wife tell Sid Shuford's gal that her husband was there when the fight took place, and that he said that they slung each other around in the bushes right considerable."

The lawyer glared at the witness, and said curtly:

"You may stand down, sir!"

His Means of Travel

"The late General William H. Payne, who died in Washington recently, saw four years' brilliant service in the Confederate Army and then returned to his home in Warrenton, Virginia, at the close of the Civil War, to take up the practice of law," says Senator Daniel, who was an intimate friend of General Payne.

"General Payne made quite a name for himself as a skilful handler of those touchy brethren —Virginia mountaineers—and was quite famous for his easy method of gentling them along and getting what he wanted out of them. On one occasion, however, he struck a tartar in the shape of an old mountaineer and the result of the tilt between them maddened General Payne to the point of explosion and upset the rest of the court room so that it was half an hour before the judge could restore order.

"At that time General Payne was prosecuting attorney and was trying a murder case. The mountaineer in question came down to testify, he having been a witness to the shooting, which occurred near his home, about fifteen miles from Warrenton.

"'You say you came down from your home this morning?' suggested General Payne, when the witness took the stand.

"'Yes, sir.'

"'You rode down on horseback, I suppose?'

"'No, sir.'

"'You drove down?'

"'No, sir.'

"'You walked down, then?'

"'No, sir.'

"'Then you came down on the train?' suggested General Payne, who was growing irritated at the titter that had followed each laconic negative from the mountaineer.

"'No, sir, I didn't come on no kyars.'

"'Well, then, sir,' exclaimed the irate lawyer, 'if you neither rode horseback, nor drove, nor walked, nor came on the cars, would you kindly tell the judge and jury how you did come?'

"'I rid one of Bill Furns's old mules,' was the solemn reply, which was drowned by the shouts of laughter from all present but General Payne and the witness."

One Asset Overlooked

H. Gerald Chapin, editor of *The American Lawyer*, takes considerable delight in telling how he was once foiled by a woman whom he was examining as a witness in supplementary proceedings.

"I had been admitted to the bar but a short time, and was a fair specimen of the average theory-stuffed, practice-wanting, law-school graduate. How joyously were the commands of the managing clerk obeyed! Here was the looked-for-opportunity to demonstrate my ability in the noble art of searchingly examining a recalcitrant witness. Of the two, I fancy, however, that it was the lady who was the more self-possessed when the proceedings opened. She was a dressmaker, and had been sued by a dry-goods firm. The examination dragged its slow length along, revealing no assets, until finally came the *omnium gatherum* query asked as a finisher.

"'Have you any property of any kind or nature, real or personal, or any right or interest in property which you have failed to mention?'

"Perhaps it was my tone she disliked. At all events, her eyes snapped.

"'Well, I've got what perhaps you wouldn't call an interest, but it's almost as good. It's an expectation. Must I answer?'

"'If you please.'

"'Well, you see, it's this way. I've got two sisters, and both of 'em have married finely. Now, neither of 'em begins to be as good looking as I am.'

"'Yes?'

"'Well, I really don't see why I shouldn't have the same show.'

"Needless to say, no receiver was appointed to administer this 'asset.'"

An Insufficient Evidence

Senator Spooner, who particularly likes to tell stories showing the humorous side of legal proceedings, relates the following with reference to an Irishman in Chicago who was being examined as to his knowledge of a certain shooting affair in that city.

"Did you," asked the presiding magistrate of the witness, "did you see the shot fired?"

"Oi did not, sir," responded the Celt, "but Oi heard it foired."

"That evidence is not satisfactory," replied

the magistrate sternly; "you may step down."

The witness left the box. No sooner had he turned his back to the judge than he gave vent to a somewhat derisive laugh.

Enraged at this contempt of court, the magistrate called the Irishman back to the witness-box. "How dare you laugh in that manner in court!" demanded the judge, angrily.

"Did you see me laugh, your honor?" asked the Irishman.

"No, but I distinctly heard you laugh," came from the irate judge.

"Sich evidence is not satisfactory," rejoined the Celt quietly, a twinkle coming into his eye.

Whereupon, says Mr. Spooner, every one in court laughed, including the magistrate.

Off and On

A lawyer noted for his success on cross-examination found his match in a certain trial, when he asked a long-suffering witness how long he had worked at his business of tin-roofing. The answer was: "I have worked at it off and on, but have worked at it steady for the past twelve years."

"How long off and on have you worked at it?"

"Sixty-five years."

"How old are you?"

"Sixty-five."

"Then you have been a tin-roofer from birth?"

"No, sir; of course I haven't."

"Then why do you say that you have worked at your trade sixty-five years?"

"Because you asked how long off and on I had worked at it. I have worked at it off and on sixty-five years—twenty years on and forty-five off."

Here there was a roar in the court room, but not at the expense of the witness, and his inquisitor hurriedly finished his examination in great confusion.

Once Was Enough

During a trial which once took place in the Court of Common Pleas at Providence, Rhode Island, the plaintiff was being examined rather sharply by the defendant's attorney. The case was one of damages claimed on account of serious bodily injuries received by plaintiff on a railroad, due, the plaintiff claimed, to the negligence of the defendant railroad company's servants. Mr. L——, the railroad company's lawyer, is noted for his nervous manner in examining witnesses, and endeavoring to disconcert and break them down. This witness, however, was determined not to be "sat down upon" by his opponent's counsel. After becoming thoroughly incensed by the attacks of the lawyer, he remonstrated. He said: "Mr. L——, I am an invalid. I will not allow you to question me in this manner. It is a positive injury to my nervous system, which is at best in a shattered condition. I shall have to refuse to answer your questions unless you put them in a different manner. I am troubled (on account of the injury received on the railroad) with sclerosis of the spinal cord, and this minute *I can see you double*, when, Lord knows, it is enough to upset a man *to see you once*."

Caught a Tartar

Browbeating lawyers sometimes find their match in female witnesses. We recall an instance in which a member of the Charleston (South Carolina) Bar, Colonel H——, was quietly but effectually "squelched" by a lady whose evidence was very damaging to his client. He realized this, and being also nettled by the imperturbability of her manner, he resolved to embarrass her if he possibly could. So he said:

"Madam, I observe that in giving your testimony you make frequent use of the word irony. May I ask if you understand its true meaning?"

"I think I do, sir," she replied. "Let me illustrate. If I were to call you a gentleman, I should unquestionably be indulging in irony."

The colonel winced visibly under this sharp thrust, the audience applauded, the jurymen laughed, and even the judge on the bench smiled, while the colonel's professional associates, who had often been bulldozed by him, keenly enjoyed his discomfiture. To add to his chagrin, the colonel lost his case.

A Darky Witness

A mulatto was on trial for murder. Among the State's witnesses was an old darky who answered to the name of George Washington. His evidence was strong against the prisoner, and the celebrated Mr. Brough desired to weaken it by throwing ridicule on the old negro.

Lawyer B. "So your name is George Washington?"

Witness. "Yes, sah, dat be my 'pellation."

Lawyer. "Where did you get that 'pellation?"

Witness. "'Way down in ole Virginny, sah."

Lawyer. "From whom did you get it?"

Witness. "Well, now you hab me, boss. Dunno."

Lawyer. "Are you a son of General George Washington, the father of his country?"

Witness. "Well, I s'pec' I be. If he was de fodder ob all dis country, he must hab ben de fodder ob de black folks as well as de fodder ob de white folks."

Lawyer. "Don't you know that the great George Washington never told a lie?"

Witness. "Dat's what um say, and in dis 'ticular I much 'sembles him, fo' I nebber tole no lies in de whole course ob my bressed life, sah."

Lawyer. "And you have told no lie about this case?"

Witness. "Why, bress de Lord! no, honey, no; I's tole nuffin' but de whole trufe."

Lawyer. "Couldn't you have made some *mistakes* in your testimony?"

Witness. "Dunno 'bout dat. We all be po' sinners here below, and I's one ob dem fellows here below, shuah; an' I's a sinner, shuah."

Lawyer. "You are a good witness for the State, Mr. George Washington, and I want to call your attention to the facts."

Witness. "T'ank you, sah, fo' de compliment; but you can't fool dis niggah. I's great on de fac's; I knows dem all fust rate, sah."

Lawyer. "Please state how long a time elapsed between the act of Bill Perkins's throwing the knife over the table at the body of the deceased, and the deceased's calling Bill Perkins a scoundrel and liar. Be particular about this."

Witness. "Well, boss, I didn't hab no watch —I's not able to carry one. And if I had one at such a 'larmin' time, I shouldn't look at it to count de minutes an' de seconds; but if my memory be jes so, it be my 'pinion dere was s'ficient time 'tween times fo' dat murderin' Bill Perkins to *demediate* and *preliberate;* dere was plenty time, in my 'pinion, fo' murder in de fust degree to be hatched out."

Mr. Brough saw he was not eliciting anything favorable from the darky, who seemed in his peculiar way to be posted in the law, so he said:

"We don't desire your legal opinion, Mr. George Washington. You're no lawyer. You may leave the stand."

Witness. "Bress de Lord, I'm not one ob de perfession. I wouldn't tell as many lies as dey do fo' de whole world. T'ank you, sah; I be glad to gib up *my* place to de next *gemman.*"

Thanks to Mr. Brough's eloquence, Mr. William Perkins was convicted of murder in the second degree, and therefore escaped the hanging so much desiderated by the good colored G. Washington.

Negative

The following dialogue recently occurred in one of our rural justices' courts :

"Do you know the prisoner, Mr. Jones?"

"Yes, to the bone."

"What is his character?"

"Didn't know he had any."

"Does he live near you?"

"So near that he has spent only five shillings for firewood in eight years."

"Did he ever come into collision with you in any matter?"

"Only once, and then he was drunk, and mistook me for a lamp-post."

"From what you know of him, would you believe him under oath?"

"That depends upon circumstances. If he was so much intoxicated that he did not know what he was saying, I would; if not, I wouldn't."

The Witness Agreed With the Lawyer

Judge Monroe, of Louisville, Kentucky, vouches for the following legal anecdote, illustrating the manner in which a browbeaten witness will sometimes retaliate upon an overbearing lawyer.

The witness in question was a farmer, and he was in court complaining that a certain neighbor had stolen some of his ducks.

"Do you know that these are your ducks?" asked the lawyer in a severe manner.

"Oh, yes, I should know them anywhere," was the confident answer, and the farmer proceeded to give in detail the various points and marks by which the birds might be identified.

"But these ducks are no different from any other ducks," objected the lawyer. "I have a good many in my yard at home just like them. What have you to say to that, sir?"

The farmer uncrossed his legs, crossed them again, expectorated, shifted his quid, and remarked with an inimitable Long Island drawl: "That's not unlikely. These are not the only ducks I have had stolen in the last few weeks!"

Amid a roar of laughter the smart lawyer sat down.

A Flat Answer

An old lawyer tells this story of one of his earliest experiences in cross-examination :

The witness seemed to be disposed to dodge his question.

" Sir," said Lynbrook, sternly, " you need not state your impressions. We want the facts. We are competent to form our own impressions. Now, sir, answer me categorically."

From that time on he could get little more than " yes " and " no " out of the witness.

Presently the lawyer said :

" You say you live next door to the defendant ? "

" Yes."

" To the north of him ? "

" No."

" To the south ? "

" No."

" Well, to the west, then ? "

" No."

" Ah," said the lawyer, sarcastically, " we are likely at last to get down to the one real fact. You live to the east of him, do you ? "

" No."

" How is that, sir ? " the astonished attorney asked. " You say you live next door to him, yet he lives neither to the north, south, east nor west of you. What do you mean by that, sir?"

"I thought perhaps you were competent to form the impression that we live in a French flat," said the witness, calmly; "but I see I must inform you that he lives next door above me."

CHAPTER III

The Witty Attorney

How the Case Was Won

SECRETARY SHAW has a keen appreciation of wit, and during his long career in the court room where he says "wit is made," he has gathered up a collection of incidents and stories of which a laugh is always the termination. Here is one he told the other day in a moment of leisure:

An old Iowa practitioner, a lawyer of ability and an orator of reputation, was pitted against a recent graduate in the profession in the trial of a case before a jury. The young lawyer had the first say, and in making his address to the jury he took particular pains to imitate certain mannerisms of the old lawyer. He carefully adjusted his cuffs before beginning his argument, stroked an imaginary imperial on his chin, and then rested the index finger of his right hand along the side of his nose. These were the habitual preliminary mannerisms of the older lawyer, and as they were repeated several times throughout the argument which was made by the young man they provoked the jury and judge to laughter.

When the veteran arose to make reply he did not neglect to go through his preliminary motions with even more deliberation and precision than usual. He bowed to the judge and to the jury, and then began:

"Gentlemen of the jury and honorable sir, that young man acts like a good lawyer, but he talks like a blamed fool."

The advantage which the young man thought he had gained in the contest vanished in the roar of laughter which followed at his expense.

Some Unexpected Evidence

Mrs. Neiswanger of Beloit sued the Missouri Pacific Company for $10,000 damages for injuries received in a fall for which, she alleged, the company was responsible. The case was tried in Rooks County.

B. P. Waggener wanted to prove that there was a full moon at the time the accident happened and to place the responsibility on the plaintiff. He sent a boy down town to a drugstore to get an almanac of that year. Without examining it, except to see that it contained the proof which he desired, he offered it in evidence.

The attorney for Mrs. Neiswanger, in his argument, said that the defendant company was the property of Jay Gould and other millionaires, who had amassed fortunes amounting to hundreds of millions. Mr. Waggener protested against this line of discussion, declaring that there was nothing in the evidence to warrant the statement.

"But there is, may it please your honor," the other lawyer declared. "It is in the evidence offered by Mr. Waggener himself."

"Where?" exclaimed Mr. Waggener.

"In this almanac," the opposing lawyer said, and sure enough in the book were pictures and short sketches of Jay Gould, Russell Sage, Henry Marquand and other associates of Gould, and every one of them said to be worth from $75,000,000 to $100,000,000.

The jury returned a verdict of $5,000 for Mrs. Neiswanger.

He Wasn't Quite Sure

It was comparatively but a short time ago that the old rules of the English courts were in full force and vigor in the conservative state of South Carolina. Thus it was distinctly provided that each attorney and counselor, while engaged in a trial, must wear "a black gown and coat." But on one occasion James L. Pettigrue, one of the leaders of the bar, appeared dressed in a light coat.

"Mr. Pettigrue," said the judge, "you have on a light coat. You cannot speak, sir."

"May it please the court, your honor," Pettigrue replied, "I conform to the law."

"No, Mr. Pettigrue, you have on a light coat. The court cannot hear you."

"But, your honor," insisted the lawyer, "you misinterpret. Allow me to illustrate. The law says that a barrister must wear 'a black gown and coat,' does it not?"

"Yes," replied the judge.

"And does your honor hold both the gown and the coat must be black?"

"Certainly, Mr. Pettigrue, certainly, sir," answered his honor.

"And yet it is also provided by law," continued Mr. Pettigrue, "that the sheriff must wear 'a cocked hat and sword,' is it not?"

"Yes, yes," was the somewhat impatient answer.

"And does the court hold," questioned Pettigrue, "that the sword must be cocked as well as the hat?"

"Eh—er—h'm," mused his honor, "you—

er—may—er—continue your speech, Mr. Pettigrue."

An Arkansas Hand

A gentleman prominent in the judiciary of North Carolina mentions a statement once made in one of the courts of that state during the progress of a case. In his address to the jury, ex-Governor ———, who is something of a wag, stated that the plaintiff was playing at a game of "bluff," and that, although he had not so much as a "pair of deuces" in his hand, he bragged as if he had an "Arkansas flush" (three jacks and a bowie-knife). The counsel opposed, in replying to this technical allusion, said: "Gentlemen of the jury, it is evident that the Arkansas hand is held by the defendant. You can see that the witness N—— is equal to a two-edged bowie-knife, and *every one knows that Governor ——— is equal to more than three knaves!*"

A New Creed

The late United States Attorney-General, Benjamin Harris Brewster, known far and wide as a brilliant lawyer and orator, thoroughly understood human nature and the dominant traits of the founders of his native Quaker city.

One day he had to try a case involving a disputed title to some property in Philadelphia, wherein was displayed much animosity on both sides and much stubbornness. The parties opposed to Brewster were all members of the Society of Friends.

At recess some of the points of the case were gone over, and the Quaker peculiarities of temperament were alluded to.

Said one lawyer to Mr. Brewster:

"As a native Philadelphian, Brother Brewster, can you tell me what those peculiar people believe in?"

"I can," was the prompt and emphatic response. "They believe in irredeemable ground rents!"

New England Wit

Essex County, Massachusetts, aside from its legal notables, like Rufus Choate, Caleb Cushing, Judge Story, Hon. Otis P. Lord, and the rest of that illustrious line who made their homes within its limits, has also been remarkable for some of its minor officers of the law, particularly its deputy-sheriffs, the majority of whom have served many years with great faithfulness and dignity, and among whom a strong friendship exists. One, Daniel Potter, always mingled with his severe devotion to official duty a keen wit and a readiness at repartee which made him a favorite with the host of acquaintances his long career brought to him. One day he entered a newspaper office in Salem, and, addressing the only scribe who was in sight, said, "I thought that I would tell you that to-morrow I shall go where I never went before and can never go again." The scribe, knowing his caller, "gave it up," and then Mr. Potter said, "It is into my eightieth year."

Once he entered the office of a prominent lawyer in a hurried manner, and addressing the lawyer in a quick tone, said, "K——, I want you to tell me, is it legal for a man to marry his *widow's sister?*"

"Why," said the attorney, "that question never occurred to me before. I'll look it up." He started to reach a legal tome from a high shelf—in fact, had his hand upon a book, when the drift of the question flashed upon him, and the book of law quickly flew from the attorney's hand at the head of the deputy-sheriff disappearing through the office doorway.

More Head

A dull judge of the inferior courts of a certain state, having attended to a variety of cases in the morning, went to dine at a friend's house with a most excellent appetite. Among the company was a witty barrister. The judge, eating very heartily of a dish of salmon, observed that he had filled himself so full that he needed hooping.

"Your honor is much more in want of heading," replied the witty barrister.

Hannibal Hamlin's Joke

When Hannibal Hamlin, of Maine, was practicing law in Bangor, he laid the foundation of a reputation for wit and joking propensities which it took him a great many years to live down.

Just previous to the year when he was to run for Congress, there came a very dull day in the Circuit Court. There were none but prosy dry-as-dust cases called, and judge, jury, counsel, and spectators were heartily bored.

So, on the spur of the moment, during a lull in the proceedings, Hamlin arose to make a motion. Those present were in a frame of mind when anything was welcome to relieve the tedium of the session.

There was a member from the back country district who always wore his hair well oiled and parted with great exactness. So straight was the line of the parting that it always seemed as if a surveyor could not have laid it out with greater nicety.

Upon this member Hamlin's eye fell as he glanced around the chamber in search of a subject, and, getting up, he said:

"Your honor, the gentleman from ——— has three hairs on the right hand side of the parting of his hair which are out of plumb. We know that the gentleman is unaware of this, and we are also equally aware of the painful embarrassment that it will cause him now that he is informed. I therefore move that this honorable body do take a ten minutes' recess in order to enable the honorable member from ——— to restore his hair to its normal condition."

Redundancy

"The counsel for the plaintiff," once said a gay and festive attorney of the Superior Court, "has been somewhat discursive in his remarks to you. He has alluded to almost everything in the pages of history, ancient and modern. He has socked with old Socrates, roamed with old Romulus, ripped with old Euripides, and canted with old Cantharides. But, gentlemen of the jury, what has that to do with this case? All his allegations are false, and the old alligator knows it himself. My client doesn't need any of this fine talk. Look at him, gentlemen, and say, if you can, that he hasn't done the honest thing by the plaintiff! From his youth up he has been as you now find him—A No. 1, extra inspected, scaled and screened, copper-fastened, free from scoots, silver-steel, buck-horn handle, nine yards to the dollar, thread thrown in!"

First of April Retorts

A little triangular piece of legal wit was perpetrated in the clerk's office of the Supreme Court of the United States, at Washington, one "All-fools' Day," between a distinguished Senator from Wisconsin, Mr. Middleton, the clerk, and the able and witty ex-Attorney-General of the United States, from New York.

"Mr. Middleton," said Senator Carpenter, "there is no statute of the United States that prohibits a man from making a fool of himself."

"Nor any *decision* of this court," gravely rejoined the clerk.

"And certainly," quickly added Mr. Evarts, with a sly twinkle of the eye, "there is nothing in the *practice* of this court to warrant any other conclusion."

Absolutely Alone

In 1867, Judge F—— held the Butler County circuit, or district court, in Iowa. One, John O'Hagan, was under indictment for assault with intent to commit great bodily harm. The evidence showed that the defendant had discovered that the complainant had gathered a load of wood, defendant's timber, which he was removing on an ox-sled; that on the instant he approached the complainant, a gray-headed man, with a gun, and threatened him with condign punishment. The State was represented by a gentleman who indulged in the following flight: "Now, gentlemen of the jury, mark the hideousness of the offense: in the depths of the primeval forest, in the silent aisle of the dim woods, while all nature was shrouded in the white ermine of winter, this poor old man, whose head was whitened with the frosts of many winters, having with tremulous fingers succeeded in gathering a few fagots to warm his thin blood, was accosted by the prisoner, with a murderous weapon, with fire in his eye and blood in his heart—without a single witness—*no other human being there save the Creator, the oxen and the sled!*"

A Short Journey

"I do not ask you, gentlemen of the jury," said an unfledged member of the bar, "to go back with me through the immeasurable vista of bygone centuries and examine the explorations and resources of science; I do not ask you to accompany the astronomer into the starry firmament, or to discover the secrets of creation! No, gentlemen, I want nothing of that! I only ask you to start with me from the county jail, and travel two miles and a half on the road toward Belmont Corner!"

Excessive Damages

A certain New England lawyer was trying a case against the city of Lawrence for a stout woman of rather unprepossessing appearance. Right behind the foreman sat a colored juryman weighing perhaps three hundred pounds. The defect in the street was very slight, and the colored man evidently took no stock in the claim. Argument, persuasion, and pathos were alike lost on him. Then the lawyer, who is rather a small-sized man, said: "Mr. Foreman, the defect was very slight, but the streets of a city should be safe for all classes of people, the rich and the poor, the old and the young, the slight and the stout. You are slender, and if you had been there you would not have fallen, but you see that the gentleman behind you and I *are just about of a build.* Now we and this poor woman have just as good a right in the street as you have." The negro's face brightened up, and when the jury retired he persistently voted for a million dollars' damages, until he was at last induced to agree with the others on a moderate verdict.

A Personal Appeal

There is a lawyer in Boston who is in the habit at times of addressing individual jurymen when inattentive or restless, and sometimes his *argumentum ad hominem* is effective. Some time ago he was trying a case against a street railway company, and there was an old sailor on the jury who seemed to give no heed to what either counsel said. The lawyer made his most eloquent appeals, but all in vain. Finally he stopped in front of the sailor and said: "Mr. Juryman, I will tell you just how this happened. The plaintiff was in command of the outward-bound open car, and stood on her starboard channels. Along came the inward-bound closed car, and just as their bows met she jumped the track, sheered to port, knocked the plaintiff off, and ran over him." The sailor was all attention after this version of the affair, and joined in a $5,000 verdict for the injured man.

The Wit of Rufus Choate

A striking example of Rufus Choate's humor, and of his marvelous faculty of so emphasizing a point that the jury could see it clear back to the roots of their optic nerves, is contained in the following passage from his summing-up in the famous Tirrell case:

To appreciate the point of the passage, we must know that Roxbury adjoins Boston. A witness against the prisoner (whom Choate was defending), having been absent, was called out of time and after the defense was all in.

Commenting upon this procedure, Mr. Choate said:

"Where was this tardy and belated witness that he comes here to tell us all that he knows, and much that he doesn't know, eight and forty hours after the evidence for the defense has been closed? Is the case so obscure that he has never heard of it? Was he ill, or in custody? Was he in Europe, Asia, or Africa? Was he on the Red Sea, or the Yellow Sea, or the Black Sea, or the Mediterranean Sea? Was he at Land's End or John O'Groat's northern boundary, drawing and defining that much vexed line? Or was he with General Taylor and his army, or wherever the fleeting southwestern boundary-line of this expanding country may at any time happen to be?

"No, gentlemen, he was at none of these places, comparatively easy of access; but—and I would emphasize upon your attention, Mr. Foreman, the fact, and urge it upon your consideration—he was in that more incontiguous, more inaccessible region, so hard to come at, and from which so few travelers return,—in short, gentlemen, he was in *Roxbury!*"

A Fighting Church

Lawyer C——, of southeastern Massachusetts, was well known for his ready wit and repartee, as well as for his skill as an attorney and eloquence as an advocate.

On one occasion in the United States Court sitting in Boston, the learned Mr. Justice Story presiding, the following colloquy took place between Mr. C—— and a witness under cross-examination:

"Mr. Witness, where did you get that book which you hold in your hand?"

"It is the book of records of the church at Beech Woods, where I reside."

"Yes, I know; but where did you get the book itself?"

"Well, I was clerk of a military company at Beech Woods, and I bought this book to keep the records of the company. Afterward the company ran down, and I was chosen clerk of the church; so I took the same book to keep the church records in."

"Ah! I see. Then that book seems to contain the records of the church *militant!*"

Some Stories of Roger Sherman

Roger M. Sherman, of Fairfield, Connecticut, was one of the ablest men this country has ever produced. He was very eminent at the bar sixty years ago, and was not surpassed by any one except Mr. Webster. He was often pitted in courts against Judge Daggett. One day Mr. Sherman, while on his legs arguing a case, was bothered in finding a reference that he wanted. Judge Daggett, to bother him more, said, "Take my spectacles."

"No, thank you," said Mr. Sherman; "no truth was ever discovered with *your* spectacles."

Sherman was once on a case where the presiding judge was a pompous man with little ability, who had been lifted to his station on his father's shoulders. This judge found some fault with Mr. Sherman for his frequent quoting from English authorities, and, as one of these precedents was about being read, remarked, "You need not take the trouble to read any more of those, so far as I am concerned."

"Well, then," said Mr. Sherman, a little warmly, "with your honor's permission I will read it to the jury; and, before I read it, let me say it is the opinion of Lord Ellenborough, a Chief Justice of England, who rose to the woolsack by his own merits, and who shone by no reflected light."

To opposing counsel Sherman was uniformly fair. He avoided, as a rule, sarcasm and personal allusion; but when pushed hard in this direction he would throw off a keen retort, in a sort of parenthesis, or as if brushing away an insect, and with unruffled self-poise pursue his consummate, clean-cut, convincing, impregnable logic. On one occasion when he had quoted to point an illustration the familiar lines from "Hudibras,"

> "distinguish and divide
> A hair 'twixt south and southwest side,"

the opposing counsel, Judge Daggett, plucked a

hair from his wig, and pretended to bisect it with his penknife. Sherman turned for a single instant to remark, "I did not say a *bristle*, sir," and continued the majestic march of his argument.

An effort had been made to remove the court from Haddam, and during the trial Sherman testified to the inconvenience of the town as a county-seat, stating, among other objections, that when he drove up there to attend court he was obliged to put up at one place and his horse at another. To which Hungerford slyly replied (as much to Mr. Sherman's amusement as his own) that he had "never before heard it urged that it was necessary for the due administration of justice for a lawyer and his horse to put up together."

The Tail of Procrastination

An advocate should be a successful pilot to conduct his bark amid the shoals that encompass him. Whatever else he may be, he should never be prosy. One eminent jurist characterized a long-drawn speech of a certain lawyer as "the last hair on the tail of procrastination."

Did Not Wish Interruptions

The most annoying specimen of the *genus judex* is the interrupting judge. We have him in every jurisdiction and in every clime. He has usually been a fairly successful trial lawyer prior to his elevation to the bench, the result of which is that he is firmly convinced that he could try every case brought before him much better than the counsel in charge. At the opening of the trial he will fidget for about ten minutes and then boldly break in and proceed to examine and cross-examine witnesses himself. Sometimes he uses the plea of "saving the court's time"; more often he does not furnish even that excuse.

"I should like to know," a counselor once said to such a one, "whether your honor has put that question for the other side or for our benefit; because, if it is in behalf of my opponent, I deny its relevancy, and, if it is for us, we don't want it."

CHAPTER IV

Slips of Speech

When Justice Harlan Forgot

A KENTUCKIAN tells a story at the expense of Justice John M. Harlan of the Supreme bench. "While I was in Washington," he said, "I met the famous jurist at a reception. The hostess was serving the punch and rallied the justice about his failure to drink more than one glass. He replied that he felt disloyal when he drank 'his' other than straight. He took a second, however, saying that he did not have any of the genuine at that time. I sent him up a case of my best the next day. On Sunday morning I attended the Presbyterian Church in Washington where Justice Harlan is an elder. The church is an old one and long steps lead up to the entrance. I was standing on the outside after the service when Justice Harlan started down the steps. In a voice that could be heard a square he shouted to me, 'That was fine,' and then, remembering where he was, he added hastily, 'The sermon, I mean.'"

Sustained in One Point

Andrew H. Green, "the father of Greater New York," took a serious view of life and was little given to humor. Nevertheless, he could appreciate a joke, and none the less if it was on himself—which some may say was proof in itself that he was not a humorist. To an acquaintance he said, apropos of something that came up in the conversation:

"That reminds me of my first case. I had been retained to defend a man in an action for damages. I was young and bumptious. The plaintiff's presentation was short, and I didn't get much chance. When that side rested I rose and with the utmost confidence, made three or four different motions, one after the other. Each was overruled by the judge as soon as made, and on entirely just grounds, as I have since come to see. I then began a laboriously-prepared address.

"'Your honor,' I commenced, 'my unfortunate client ——'

"'There the court is with you,' came from the bench in the gentlest of tones."

Emory Storrs's Bluebird

A pair of ex-jurors were swapping recollections in New York one day. The retired member of the brace agreed with the one who expects to serve some more that there had been cases in which jurors were not altogether constrained to go according to the evidence.

"I was some years ago on the jury that tried Jere Dunn for killing Jim Elliott, the prize-fighter, in Chicago," said the retired one. "Jere Dunn was a Beau Brummel gambler. Jim Elliott was—well, he was a prize-fighter.

"The killing occurred in a questionable resort. There was nothing in the case that appealed to a New Englander such as I am. When all the evidence was in I didn't know how I stood. It was a case of six and six.

"Dunn's lawyer was Emory Storrs, the brilliant, erratic Storrs, the great criminal lawyer of his day.

"In his peroration Storrs said, as well as I remember the words: 'Gentlemen of the jury, acquit Jere Dunn, and to-morrow the sun will shine brighter, and the bluebirds will sing more joyously.'

"Now when I was a young man in Connecticut the woods were full of bluebirds and robins and other plumaged species, but the bluebird was my favorite. I killed robins and sparrows and other things that had feathers, but I never harmed a bluebird.

"Storrs's reference to the bluebirds touched me. When the jury retired we were all about of one mind, and Jere Dunn was acquitted.

"Some months later I was at the banquet which Emory Storrs gave to Henry Irving and I told Storrs about the few lines in his defense of Dunn that caught me.

"'That was very good of you,' he said, 'but I made an awful slip in that sentence. If you know anything about a bluebird you know it can't sing any more than a cow.'

"Then I remembered that I had never heard a bluebird sing.

"Sir Henry Irving, the tragedian, was among the listeners to this story. He laughed, and said, in his most gracious manner:

"'I presume the barrister referred to the bluebird he was asking the jury to release.'"

Chronic Disability

The lawyer was examining him concerning his qualifications as a juror.

"Have you ever served on a jury?" he asked.

"No, sir," answered the man. "I've been drawn a good many times, but I was always too smart to get caught on a jury."

"What's that, sir?" interrupted the judge,

sternly. "Do you boast of your smartness in escaping jury duty?"

"No, your honor," said the man. "Not at all. When I said I was too smart I meant that I was always excused because the lawyers thought I wasn't ignorant enough."

A Warm Reception

A man was on trial for stealing a pig. The owner testified to finding a similar pig, taking it home, and setting it loose in the presence of the bereaved porcine ancestress. "Well," said the solicitor for the State, "how did the sow receive it?"

"*With outstretched arms,* sir!" triumphantly replied the witness.

What Sex?

Some weeks since, the case of a sister of a man deceased against the administrators came up in one of our circuit courts. The plaintiff brought suit for twenty-six hundred dollars, amount claimed for thirteen years' service, during which time she had attended to and taken care of her brother, who had died without rewarding her pecuniarily for her really invaluable devotion.

There being a great number of cases in court,

by consent of counsel, the matter was submitted to three referees, who, after hearing the arguments *pro* and *con*, were to decide whether the bill should be allowed or not. At the appointed time the room was crowded with spectators, and no little interest was manifested in the result. The counsel for the plaintiff, a sedate and solemn man, concluded that the best way to secure his ends was by adopting the pathetic. Accordingly he began:

"Gentlemen, for thirteen long years did my client devote herself to her unfortunate brother. With an affection such as only a sister can feel did she minister to his every want. Patiently, faithfully she toiled, never complaining, never unwilling, never murmuring. And never was she rewarded, except in that inward consciousness of having done a noble and self-sacrificing deed. Yes, gentlemen, for thirteen long years she toiled and labored, and during that time she never received enough to *buy her a pair of pantaloons!*"

The perfect simplicity of this forgetfulness of his client's sex was so apparent, and the mistake so natural, the flight from the pathetic to the broad ridiculous was so sudden and complete that the effect can scarcely be imagined.

CHAPTER V

At the Expense of the Bench

A Good Lawyer

SOME years ago a colored citizen was arraigned for petty larceny before the Court of General Sessions of Sussex County, Delaware, presided over by the learned Chief Justice Gilpin, a gentleman of small stature, with gray beard and mustache. The ebony party, on being asked if he had counsel, replied that he had not —he was too poor to employ one; and, besides, he had no witnesses. Whereupon Judge Gilpin, turning to the Attorney-General, said, with a smile: "I will conduct the defense," and called for the indictment. The trial proceeded, the prisoner duly cared for by the judge. No case being made out, Sambo was told by the judge that he was free to go where he pleased. "Thank you," said the freeman; and as he retired from the presence he was met at the door by his friend Bill, who asked what lawyer he had. "Well, I don't know his name," replied Sam, "but it was that little gray-whiskered fellar sittin' up there in the middle, and a deuced good little 'un he is too ! "

Jim and the Judge

Jim Webster was brought before a Western judge for fowl-stealing. After the evidence had been given, the justice, with a perplexed look, said: "But I do not understand, Webster, how it was possible for you to steal those fowls when they were roosting right under the owner's window and there were two vicious dogs in the yard."

"It wouldn't do yer a bit of good, jedge, for me to 'splain how I cotched dem chickens, for yer couldn't do it yerself if yer tried it forty times, and yer might get yer hide full of buck-shot. De best way for yer to do, jedge, is for yer to buy yer chickens in de market, like uder folks do, and wen yer wants ter commit any rascality, do it on de bench, whar yer am at home ! "

An Eye For Justice

Representative Dougherty, of Missouri, knows a sheriff in one of the counties of his district named "Jack" Steele, who is somewhat of a joker.

At a recent session of court Steele summoned a panel of jurors and picked out the fattest men he could get.

After the first case they were hearing was well under way, Steele took the jury to a local hotel and fed them liberally on cabbage, buttermilk and other sleep-inducing viands. The result was that every juror went to sleep that afternoon, and most of them snored, to the great discomfort of the judge.

"Mr. Sheriff," the judge said, after the jury had been awakened, "I will not submit to such outrages as this. Next time you summon a jury I want you to pick out men not for their girth, but with a single eye to justice."

Steele obeyed. Every man on the next panel was one-eyed.

A Guilty Judge

In these days when the toot of the automobile is so frequently heard in the land, prosecutions for violating speed ordinances are very frequent, especially in rural communities where there sometimes develops an insane hatred of the "devil wagons" and their owners and drivers.

A certain justice of the peace, not a thousand miles away from Philadelphia, who was celebrated for his severity when dealing with such cases, one day had to try a man for exceeding the speed limit of twelve miles an hour prescribed in a certain township.

The day of trial came and the justice overslept himself. The court was twenty-five miles from his house, and no train available.

So the justice hired a motor car, started off, reached the court well inside the hour, and in time to fine the twelve-mile-an-hour desperado twenty dollars and costs.

But the worm turned. Scarcely had the court been adjourned when the justice found himself served with a warrant, and the story goes that he had to open court again, hear the witnesses, and fine himself in a similar way.

Of this story it may be well remarked that it is "good enough to be true," and every lover of the horseless steed will hope that it was.

A Dependent Citizen

The following story is told of a well-known member of the bar in Alleghany County, New York, than whom there never lived a gentler, kindlier spirit. With his scholarly attainments and profound knowledge of legal lore, he possessed the simple, dependent nature of a child, and, it may be added, a child's utter guilelessness and faith in his kind.

His wife, fortunately for the worldly success of the pair, was shrewd and practical in a marked degree; upon her strong independence of character, Judge C—— leaned heavily, except within the domain of his profession, where, curiously enough, his opinions were singularly prompt and infallible. In the domestic and social circles, however, he deferred to Mrs. C—— in the simplest matters, and so habitual had this state of things become that it did not occur to either of them that there was anything unusual in it. From donning his winter flannels to leading a card at the whist table he never pretended to act without "Helen's" sanction and advice.

But one day he showed his condition of mental servitude in a really astonishing way. He was suffering from toothache, and his wife sent him to the village dentist for relief. Obediently he went, got into the chair, and opened his mouth for the preliminary examination.

"Which tooth is it aches, judge?" inquired the dentist, poising the forceps.

There was a moment's hesitation; then the judge sat up from his reclining position, and looking innocently at the dentist said, in all good faith, "Well, now, I don't know; I'll go home and ask Helen."

When the Lion Wags His Tail

Some years ago George R. Peck, formerly of Kansas, after he became general solicitor of the Chicago, Milwaukee & St. Paul Railway Company, was called to South Dakota to argue an important case before the Federal Court. He was accompanied to the seat of justice by Alfred Beard Kittredge, the local attorney of the company, who has since become a United States senator.

Mr. Peck made a fine argument and afterward walked to the hotel with the judge of the court. "I liked your argument this forenoon, Mr. Peck," the judge said: "it was a masterly presentation of your case. I don't think you left anything unsaid that could have been said."

Mr. Peck thanked the judge for the compliment and afterward went to Mr. Kittredge, elated. "I am going to win that case, Kittredge," he said. "What makes you think so?" asked Mr. Kittredge. "Why, I'll tell you on the quiet. Walking with me to the hotel to-day, the judge complimented me and added that I had left nothing unsaid."

"Oh, is that all?" Mr. Kittredge said. "Don't let him fool you by that kind of talk. We all know him here. I'll tell you a story.

"Once there was a lion tamer whose duty it was to go into the cage and put his head in a big lion's mouth twice a day. One day, after he had gotten his head in the animal's mouth, he asked the keeper in a low voice, 'Is the lion wagging his tail?' 'He is,' replied the keeper. 'Then I'm gone,' said the tamer, and the next moment the lion closed his jaws and killed the tamer."

It was both a story and a prophecy. Mr. Peck lost his case.

Mr. O'Flaherty's Precaution

The judgment held by Mr. Dunnigan against Mr. O'Flaherty had been paid in open court, but the defendant still lingered, with a dissatisfied expression clouding his face. Noticing this, the judge asked, "What are you waiting for, Mr. O'Flaherty?"

"Oi'm waitin' fer me resate."

"But the judgment has been marked satisfied, and that is much better than a receipt," explained the judge.

"Shure it's a resate oi'm wantin'," affirmed Mr. O'Flaherty.

"Don't you understand?" asked the judge. "You can't have a receipt. Your payment of the judgment is now part of the record in the case, and it will always show that you have paid."

"Oi want a resate," obstinately repeated Mr. O'Flaherty.

"You can't have a receipt, I tell you," impatiently replied the judge. "Your payment has been noted on the records, and that's better than a dozen receipts."

"But oi want a resate."

"See here, O'Flaherty, what do you mean by this infernal obstinacy?" demanded the judge.

"Yer 'anner an' mesilf'll be dyin' some o' these days," explained Mr. O'Flaherty, "an' whin oi come to the gate Saint Pether 'll be afther axin', 'Did yez pay thot Dunnigan?' An' oi'll say, 'Yis, oi did thot.' An' Saint Pether 'll say, 'Where's the resate?' An' oi'll say, 'It's sathisfied on the record, an' oi have no resate.' An' thin Saint Pether'll say: 'Go an' get a resate. Yez can't get in here widout wan.' An', yer 'anner, it's all over purgathory oi'll have to be afther trampin' to find yer 'anner an' git a resate."

Never Again

There is a certain judge in one of our higher courts who rather prides himself upon his precise knowledge of the law. One day he was compelled to listen to a case that had been appealed from one of the lower courts. The young lawyer who appeared for the appellant was long and tedious; he brought in all the elementary text-books, and quoted the fundamental legal propositions.

At length the judge thought it was time to make an effort to close the argument.

"Can we not assume," he said suavely, "that the court itself knows a little about the law?"

"That's the very mistake I made in the other court," answered the lawyer, "and I don't want to let it defeat me twice!"

Remitted His Fine

In the days antedating railroads in northern Iowa, the days of saloons and circuit courts, a certain ponderous judge was for many years accompanied on his rounds by District-Attorney Wood, popularly known as Old Timber-Wood. He had been christened Timothy, the name was curtailed to Tim, and by easy evolution developed into Timber.

Old Timber-Wood was a unique and interesting character; rough but dignified, of sound intellect, gifted with a keen sense of humor, and far surpassing in mental acumen his professional superior, whom, however, he usually treated before the world with an almost ostentatious deference. They were the warmest of friends, the feeling between them was romantically tender, notwithstanding that they had frequent and violent public fallings out.

The judge, who was entirely lacking in personal dignity, really needed the support of his friend's deferential attitude to keep him in countenance, and when it was temporarily removed, Old Timber-Wood's love of satire occasionally betraying him into the sacrilege known as "contempt of court," he was stung to fury, and promptly punished the offense. Many a fine had the attorney been subjected to for his incautious witticisms. Being in a constant state of impecuniosity, he invariably applied to the judge himself for money to pay these assessments, a favor which was never refused, the fact that he must humble himself to ask it sufficiently restoring his honor's complacency.

The judge was of a thirsty habit, and frequently left the bench, substituting Wood in his place—as an old-time schoolmaster substituted one of the larger boys when he wished to absent himself from the room—and stepped out to refresh himself at a neighboring saloon.

On one occasion, very shortly after a skirmish with the attorney, in which he had finally avenged his insulted dignity in the usual way, he abruptly called Wood to the bench and started down the aisle. Wood hastily slipped into his place, and before the judge had reached the door rapped sharply on the desk and called out, "Gentlemen, before proceeding further with the case, the court wishes to instruct the clerk to remit the fine lately imposed upon Attorney Wood."

The judge halted, wheeled about with a very red face, and opened his lips to protest, but the bar and the jury drowned him out with a chorus of laughter.

A Legal Hoax

Judge E. is very fond of relating most marvelous stories of his exploits, which are always accompanied by gestures equally extraordinary.

A few years ago the judge was "summering" with a couple of professional friends, who, knowing his proclivities to the use of the long bow, determined to have a little sport at his expense. In the course of their rambles they stopped at a hotel near some famous fishing grounds, and planned to start fishing at four o'clock in the morning. Judge E., not caring to go, was not to be waked when the others started.

Morning came, and the two sportsmen started,

leaving their unconscious victim slumbering peacefully. As they passed through the office of the hotel they said to the clerk, tapping their foreheads significantly, "Keep your eye on that friend of ours—he's harmless enough, but odd—and don't let him excite himself."

Of course the rumor that the new guest was "a little off" spread through the hotel, and at breakfast the judge was the centre of all observation; but supposing that it was due to the fact of his being the renowned Judge E., he was rather flattered than otherwise.

After breakfast he strolled into the office, where were assembled half a dozen of the guests, engaged in conversation about the mysterious lodger. Not noticing the looks of distrust cast upon him, he began by saying, "Fine morning, gentlemen." No one seemed to be inclined to dispute this statement, and silence reigned for a few moments.

Suddenly the judge was reminded of certain wonderful exploits, and, rising, he began an account of them, couched in the most flowery language, and to enforce his remarks laid his hand on the shoulder of his nearest auditor, who, not fancying the presence of the supposed lunatic, retired through the nearest open door with more haste than courtesy.

Somewhat disconcerted, the narrator smoked in silence for a few moments; but, unwilling that so good a story should remain untold, he advanced and resumed the tale, emphasizing it by vigorous blows on the clerk's desk.

The clerk at once deserted his post, exclaiming, "Now calm yourself, sir; just try to be calm."

"Be what?" cried the judge, thoroughly mystified.

"There, now, be calm; don't excite yourself, or we shall have to take measures to restrain you."

"Restrain me! Take measures!" fairly howled the victim of the joke, in a perfect rage. "I'd like to see you."

The clerk was now thoroughly persuaded that for his own personal safety strong measures were necessary, and was about to put his threat into execution when Judge E.'s two companions returned, and hurried explanations followed.

Judge E. could only hush the matter up by a generous "treat." Even then the story leaked out, and now the judge can be stopped in his most marvelous tale by his auditor's saying, "Now don't get excited."

Rustic Wit

In Carroll County, Arkansas, some years ago, one John Doe was put to trial upon a criminal charge, one of the Senators in Congress from Arkansas appearing as his counsel. The State's attorney was "to the manner born," imbibing with every breath of mountain air from boyhood up a love of freedom and independence, and a hearty contempt for shirt collars and the technicalities of the law.

In the progress of the trial it became necessary to prove a fact of which the records of an adjoining county were by statute made the best evidence.

Now these records had long since been destroyed by fire, and this fact was well known to judge, counsel, and public generally.

The State's attorney called a witness to prove his needed fact. Defendant's counsel objected to the evidence because it was secondary, and no foundation had been laid for its reception by proof of loss of the record, whereupon the following colloquy took place between the judge and prosecuting attorney:

Judge. "Mr. State's Attorney, before you can introduce this witness you must show the loss of the record."

State's Attorney. "I presumed your honor

was aware of the fact that the records of Marion County were burned."

Judge. "As a private citizen I do know the fact, but as the court I do not, and you must put the proof of the fact into your case."

State's Attorney. "Well, your honor, it strikes me as a little singular that your honor knows something off the bench, and don't know anything on it."

What They Said to Moriarty

Some queer things happen in the New Jersey courts sometimes. Many years ago they used to have a system by which men were appointed to the bench as judges because of their ignorance of the law. Well, these lay judges, as they were called, had a fine thing of it. It was a political job, of course, and carried the same salary as that drawn by the law judges. There was really nothing to do but to sit on the bench beside the latter and look wise. Once there was a big case on trial in Trenton and it took a week before it was finished. There were two law judges and the lay judge. The last man was a character, and I knew him well. He was a man named Moriarty, and a bricklayer by trade. We often heard him say that he only worked one week in all the year, and that was the week before election. However, he got on this case I'm telling you about, and it involved a great many technicalities and a great deal of money. I was a witness on the case, and had to be in attendance every day, and a long and dreary time I had of it. I often saw the law judges whisper together, but they never even so much as looked at Moriarty, except once, when one of them bent over and said something to him, to which he nodded profoundly. Several times after that I noticed that they made a motion as if to speak to him, but changed their minds, and I would be willing to bet that he was sound asleep at the time.

After the trial was over I traveled down to his home in Cumberland County, and stopped over night at his house. After dinner, when we were smoking on the front porch, I said to him:

"That's the first time I was ever at a trial when a lay judge presided."

"It was my first case, too."

"Did the law judges consult with you?"

"They did."

"On points of law?"

"Not exactly."

"On what then?"

"Do you remember in the middle of the

trial when there was a big fat man on the witness stand?"

"Yes."

"Well, when that man had been there two hours or more, the judge leaned over to me, and he says, says he, in a whisper: 'Whin that confounded idjit gets off the stand, we'll adjourn the court and go out and get a drink.'"

"And did they never speak to you about the case?"

"Divil a word—nor I to thim."

Squashed

Colonel M——, commonwealth's attorney for ——— County, Massachusetts, had unbounded influence over the presiding justice of the county court under the old system. B——, a young lawyer, had been retained to defend a prisoner, and discovering what he conceived to be a fatal defect in the indictment, submitted a motion to quash. He was proceeding to sustain his point as best he could when the presiding justice, a fat old fellow, settled himself in his chair and fell asleep. The argument proceeded, and at its close "the squire" roused up, and rubbing his eyes, said, "Squash 'er."

Colonel M—— was on his feet in a moment,

and inquired, with much asperity, "Do I understand this court as sustaining the motion to quash my indictment?"

"Oh! No, Kurnil," said the squire. "I squashes the motion to squash."

A Good Retort

An eminent lawyer was arguing a case before a quick-tempered judge, who grew impatient, and said:

"Your point is perfectly understood by the court; please make your argument as short as possible."

"I am making it as short as possible," said the lawyer as he proceeded.

After a few minutes the judge interrupted him again, saying, "You are taking too much time; we have many cases to hear; and I want you to understand that I am sitting here for the dispatch of business."

"I beg your pardon," said the old lawyer, bowing low. "*I thought your honor was sitting here to administer justice.*"

He was suffered to proceed.

Crime Necessary in a New Country

A mild and lenient man was old Judge ———, one of the earliest magistrates of Oakland under the first county judge system enacted by the Governor and judges. He had some peculiarities which might remind one of Dicky Riker, the famous Recorder of New York, save that Dicky grew more and more severe, and the Oakland judge more and more forgiving, as age came upon him. Yet had they points of analogy, in that each used a certain rigmarole as a sort of peroration preceding the sentence passed upon a culprit. But mark the difference:

Dicky used to say, when the prisoner was before him for sentence—no matter what the crime, even if it was eating his great-grandfather's head off—

"Prisoner, stand up. The crime of which you have been convicted is becoming very prevalent in this community, and must be put a stop to! I give you five years."

Not so the sword-and-scale bearer of Oakland. His formula of conscience and duty was different, though not less uniform—thus:

"Prisoner, hold up your hand. You have been found guilty of (larceny, assault and battery, trespass, as the case might be); but the court takes into consideration that this is a new country, society is unsettled, nor are the laws understood. We must expect such things in settling a new country. So I give you thirty days."

On one occasion a man was arraigned for willful perjury. He had property and standing, but the case was so clear that the jury pronounced him "guilty" without leaving their seats.

The prosecuting attorney was in ecstasies over what all criminal lawyers consider no small exploit—the recovery of a verdict of guilty on an indictment for perjury.

The prisoner being brought up for sentence, the judge commenced:

"You have been convicted of parjury, prisoner. This is a grave offense; but I consider that this is a new country, and we must have *some* parjury among the difficulties of settling a new country. So I shall only give you thirty days in the county jail."

The prosecuting attorney, to wind up a case of false swearing, went outside the court-house and gave vent to a large volume of the genuine article.

The Justice Swore

Up in Westchester County they tell many good anecdotes of the late Justice Barnard. His vocabulary contained strenuous words.

"I remember one story told by Isaiah Williams, an old-time lawyer who died several years ago," said a member of the Westchester bar the other day. "Williams had had a case in which the old General Term, consisting of Justices Barnard, Gilbert and Pratt, had decided against him. Judge Barnard wrote the opinion, and the other judges concurred.

"Williams was still convinced that he was in the right. Several days later he chanced upon Judge Gilbert in the street and stopped him to argue the merits of the case all over again.

"'You're right, you're right,' said Judge Gilbert, cutting him short. 'I remember your point and agree with you perfectly.'

"'Then why in thunder didn't you write a dissenting opinion and say so?' demanded the irate Williams.

"'Well, Mr. Williams,' responded Judge Gilbert, confidentially, 'you see Joe swears so.'"

CHAPTER VI

The Prisoner Retorts

Why He Jumped

"SPEAKING about curious explanations that are made in courts of justice, and the resourcefulness of men who are confronted by the rather unpleasant prospect of a sentence of a long or short duration, reminds me of a rather novel case which came under my observation some time ago," said a man who frequents the courts of a southern city, "and the particular case I have in mind shows how desperately resourceful a man may sometimes be. The charge brought against the wily prisoner in this instance is of no particular moment. The act he had committed was to plunge headlong into Bayou St. John, that romantic stream which winds a rather sluggish way into the lake in the lower part of the city. He was pulled out, and before he could thoroughly realize what was happening to him he was dripping along a public highway with a robust policeman holding him by the arm. He was lodged in jail and it became necessary for him to make some sort of explanation to go on one of the city records, and this is where the funny part of the business comes in. The recorder put the question to him bluntly: 'Why did you jump into the bayou?' The fellow hesitated for a second or so. 'Well, judge,' he finally said, with more confidence than you can imagine, 'I just wanted to find out what was at the bottom of the bayou.' The explanation was clever, and even original, but the recorder was not inclined to accept it, so he entered up a small fine against the man."

Fell in Line

One morning some thirty prisoners were lined up for hearings, and included in the bunch were several Chinamen. As the long line slowly moved toward the magistrate as case after case was disposed of, the Celestials finally came to the front. The ensuing dialogue did not differ materially from those of other cases, and was as follows:

"What's your name?" by the magistrate.

"Ah Sin," from the prisoner.

Questions as to the residence and occupation of the prisoner followed, and then this:

"You are charged with being drunk and making a disturbance down on Ninth Street."

"Yep; me dlunk."

"Ten dollars or ten days," was the way in which the case was dismissed.

The next Chinaman gave his name as Ah Lee, the charge being disorderly conduct in making a row in a restaurant. It was disposed of in the same way. The third Chinaman gave his name as Ah Hin.

"Seems to me there are a good many of you Ahs," remarked the magistrate, "and you seem to be a pretty disorderly lot. You are charged with striking a man on the street while you were drunk. How is that?"

"Yep; me hit him," was the short reply.

"Ten dollars or ten days."

The next prisoner was a big, brawny Irishman, who had been paying careful attention to the cases preceding him.

"What's your name?"

"Ah Hill!" retorted the son of Erin, wrathfully. "Phat does it matter? It's tin dollars or tin days anyway."

But he was mistaken; he got off easier.

Justice Between Friends

Ex-Representative John Allen tells of a young man in Dallas who "had occasion," as they used to say in Texas, to shoot a friend with whom he had had an altercation.

As the accused had no funds, the court designated a member of the San Antonio bar to defend him. As the jury was being selected, counsel asked his client whether he knew of any reason why any of the jurors should be challenged.

"No, I don't," was the whispered reply, "but if they find me guilty I have a brother who is game enough to challenge every last one of 'em. If you're a true friend you'll challenge the judge; but I'd like to attend to the sheriff myself!

A Narrow Escape

During a session of a West Virginia court a darky was tried for cutting a white man with a razor. His counsel wished to prove that the white man was the aggressor, and that the darky was physically unable to defend himself without a weapon. Being duly sworn, "Uncle Jim" was asked whether he had ever been injured in any way.

"Yes, sah."

"Tell the jury all about it."

"Well, sah, it was down in Chat'noogy. I's a-wukkin' down dah, an' I done fell off'n a derrick—fell sixty feet. I broke dis hyah laig, an' I fractured dis hyah ahm in two places, an' I knocked out dem two teef, an' my collah-bone was broke, an' I had three ribs busted; dis hyah yeah was tore off, an' hatter be sewed on agin; an' de fac' is, gent'men, ef it hadn't been for a pile o' bricks dat sort o' broke my fall, I'd 'a' been liable to be *hurt serious*."

His Patriotism Won His Freedom

Representative Griggs of Georgia is a *raconteur* who doesn't mind telling a joke on himself.

"When I was prosecuting attorney of Bartlett County," said Mr. Griggs yesterday, "an old fellow, not of much account but a great friend of mine, was indicted for larceny. He came to see me and protested, but I told him I must do my duty to the State.

"Well, the case came to trial and Jim had no counsel. The judge looked at him severely over his spectacles, and said:

"'Mr. Brown, you are charged with a very grave offense. I think you had better secure an attorney.'

"Old Jim got up with a preternatural gravity, and addressed the court and me.

"'Your honor,' he said, 'I love the old State of Georgy. On one of these old red hills I first seen the light of day, and when I die I hope to lay my tired old bones down right here. For no consideration would I take advantage of the good old State.'

"Here he looked hard at me, the State attorney.

"'So, your honor, until the State of Georgy gets a lawyer, I don't expect to hire one,' he added, and sat down.

"Needless to say we rewarded Brown's patriotism with freedom."

He Would Have Gotten a Lawyer

I was attending the term of Henrico court one spring (says Thomas Nelson Page) when I had been at the bar only a year or two, and was in the court room when the criminal docket was called. The clerk read out the case of the Commonwealth *vs.* Mannie Johnson, an indictment for a felony, and my attention was arrested by hearing the sheriff say the prisoner had no counsel. If there is one thing which excites the sympathy of a young lawyer, it is a prisoner who has no counsel. There was a colloquy between the judge, the commonwealth's attorney, and the sheriff, and the judge finally said, "Well, bring him in, anyhow; I will see about it."

The long-legged, gangling sheriff retired, and in a little while reentered with his most professional solemnity about him, preceded by a stumpy, rusty, bow-legged negro, about thirty-five years of age and about five feet in height, who looked as unlikely to be able to steal a steer as anybody in the world.

The sheriff roughly pointed out a chair to him, and he sat down in it without even taking a look at the jury lounging in their box.

"Is that the man?" asked the judge. "Did that man steal a steer?"

The sheriff smiled the smile of one familiar with the classes who steal steers; the commonwealth's attorney smiled with the smile of one who makes $10 out of each indictment for a felony which he is able to draw and get a grand jury to find; even the jury smiled; I think, perhaps, I smiled. The prisoner, with his old ragged hat in his hand, was the only one who did not smile. He glanced up for a second at the judge on the bench, then dropped his eyes to a level, and sat as motionless as before.

"Have you any counsel?" asked the judge. The prisoner looked at him, but said nothing; and the judge, appreciating the fact that he perhaps did not understand the question, asked him, "Have you any lawyer?"

"No, suh," he said, twisting a little in his seat, and settling down as before.

The judge turned to me and asked me to defend him, adding civilly, "If my other clients could wait a little while." I informed him that I thought my other clients could wait; that I always made my clients wait my own pleasure (they had then been waiting some months); and, going around, took a seat approximately near to my new client's side.

"Have you any witnesses?" I asked.

He did not look at me, or, if he did, it was only a glance; he simply said, "No, suh."

"Can you get any if I get a continuance—if I get the case put off till next month?"

"I don't know; no, suh," he said, scarcely taking the trouble to speak.

"Well," I said, rising, "I think we are ready; we might as well go into trial."

The jury was waked up and sworn. The clerk made the prisoner stand up, and read an indictment as long as himself, and the commonwealth's attorney called his witnesses. There were five of them.

The first was a farmer, who testified that he owned the steer in question, and that one evening he saw him in his pasture when he attended to his stock, and the following morning when he went out he missed him. He thought at first that he might have fallen into the ditch, but not finding him, he went around the fence, and finally found his tracks going out of the gate and down the road toward Richmond, followed by the tracks of a man who was evidently driving him. He got his horse and followed in hot haste, but the steer had evidently been stolen early in the night, and he did not overtake him until he got to town; there, after some hunting, he found him in the possession of a butcher, who claimed to have bought him from the negro in question.

The butcher himself was sworn, and testified that early one morning the prisoner drove the steer up to his gate, claiming it to be his, and stating that he wanted some money very badly, in consideration of which he, the butcher, gave him $15 for the steer.

The other witnesses were two men who happened to be present, and who identified the prisoner as the person who sold the butcher the steer, and the policeman who made the arrest, and who testified to something which the commonwealth's attorney called "a confession."

I asked for several instructions, which the judge, very unjustly, as I thought at the time, refused positively to give. I am bound to say now that my views upon this matter have become modified by time. I cross-examined the witnesses with much severity. Then the commonwealth's attorney made a few remarks, stating that it was not necessary to make a speech, as the evidence was all one way. And then I entered upon my argument.

I made what I deemed a very able and eloquent defense. I charged all five witnesses with perjury, and proved it to my complete satisfaction. The jury, I am bound to say, were flattering in their attention. Only a few of them dozed. When I closed, the commonwealth's attorney rose, and commented upon my argument in a way which came very near bringing on a personal collision in court between him and myself.

Then the jury retired, and returned so promptly that I felt a glow of enthusiasm that they should hesitate so short a time, even after my able defense. The clerk took the indictment and read the verdict:

"We, the jury, find the prisoner guilty, and sentence him to the penitentiary for ten years."

I was scarcely able to believe my own senses. I arose immediately, and, with some heat, moved to set the verdict aside on the ground that it was contrary to the evidence. This the judge refused to do. My client never blinked; he simply sat immobile as ever; but I was outraged. I turned to him and said,

"Well, I did the best I could for you."

He grunted, but did not look at me, and I felt that he was overcome with emotion at what I had done for him, and said:

"The only thing for us to do now is to get an appeal. I will take it up to the higher court, and fight it through for you. But it will take some money, because there are costs, and of course you ought to pay me a fee if you can. Have you got any money at all?"

Without looking at me, he said, "No, suh; ef I had, I'd 'a' got me a lawyer!"

I have become satisfied that he ought to have gone to the penitentiary, but the sheriff informed me afterward that he got out of jail that night.

CHAPTER VII

Humor of the Bench

A Witty Judge

THEY tell a story in Halifax which instances the ready wit of Judge Haliburton, the author of *Sam Slick:*

In a certain noted trial there was found some difficulty in getting a jury. One man who was claiming exemption seemed very reluctant to state the grounds for his claim. At last, when pressed, he exclaimed,

"Well, your honor, the truth is I have the itch."

"Scratch him off, Mr. Prothonotary, scratch him off," was the judge's instant response.

A Pious Wish

In a certain New Hampshire court the late Arthur Livermore was the presiding judge, and a crier was officiating for the first time after his appointment, and was not able to repeat the stated form of opening. On his utterly breaking down, the judge said: "Now, Mr. Crier, repeat after me. 'Oyez!'" and the crier repeated after the judge, sentence by sentence, through the usual proclamation. Then said the judge, "Now say, 'God save the State.'" The crier repeated, "God save the State." The judge added (*sotto voce*), "And the crier too."

Premature Death

There was once a learned judge of over eighty who never took any exercise. Not feeling very well, he consulted a physician.

"You have no business to live without taking exercise," said the physician. "You must give up your sedentary habits and walk for an hour every day."

"But it bores me so," pleaded the judge. "If I follow your advice, I shall walk myself into a premature grave."

Two Against One

Some years ago, when the late Judge M—— was holding court in one of the interior counties of Maine, a case was called which had long been in litigation. The costs considerably exceeded the amount at issue, and the judge, thinking it impracticable to keep the suit longer in court, advised the parties to refer the matter, whereupon they assented, and agreed to refer the case to three honest men. The judge said the case involved some legal points which would require one of the referees, at least, to have a knowledge of law; therefore he would suggest the propriety of their selecting one lawyer and two honest men.

A Modern Fable

The jury having returned a verdict of guilty against a man on trial for stealing sheep, his lawyer arose and said to the court:

"May it please your honor, I ask to quash all proceedings on the ground of defective information. While my client admits stealing twelve lambs, he has been charged with the theft of twelve sheep. A lamb is not legally a sheep, your honor."

"Your point is well taken," replied the judge after reflection, "and I will give the prisoner the benefit of the technicality. I was intending to sentence him to the penitentiary for two years, but will change it to the state prison for the same term. While a lamb is not a sheep, neither is a state prison a penitentiary."

Moral—It took the twelve lambs to pay the lawyer's bill.

An Apparition

A queer case occurred in the State of Louisiana. A man disappeared. He was thought to be dead, and his effects were distributed. He came back after twenty years, and went into the court issuing the decree, and asked the judge to issue an order to give him his property. The judge said, "In the eye of this court you are dead. This is not the place for you to get mistakes rectified. Get a lawyer, and he will tell you what to do." The man persisted, and said he "wanted his property, and it was an outrage to deprive him of it another day." The judge said, "I tell you that in the eye of this court you are *dead*. Sheriff, take this apparition out of court!"

Jumping at Conclusions

Two Colorado judges lately occupied the same room in a hotel near the city of Pueblo. They were greatly annoyed during the first portion of the night by a neighbor who was snoring at a terrible rate. They lay sleepless and silent for a long time, listening with a horrid fascination to the efforts of "the man who snored." Finally the sleeper made one mighty effort, and with a last convulsive, gurgling gasp relapsed into silence, which was shortly broken by one of the legal victims, who in a fervent tone exclaimed, "*Thank God, he's dead!*"

A Concise Charge

During the "Reconstruction Period," a colored man was elected a justice of the peace in the backwoods of South Carolina. His first case happened to be one in which the defendant asked for trial by jury. When the testimony was in and the arguments had been concluded, the lawyers waited for the judge to proceed with his instructions to the jury. The judge seemed somewhat embarrassed. Finally one of the lawyers whispered to him and told him that it was time for him to charge the jury. Looking warily at the jury, with a grim judicial air, the judge said:

"Gentlemen uv de jury, sence dis is a very small case, I'll jes' charge y'll a dollar an' a ha'f apiece."

"Shudgment"

A few years ago a trial was in progress in the Superior Court of Cincinnati, in which was involved the value of the chairs and furniture of a tonsorial establishment. The learned judge, to whom the case had been submitted, was at a nonplus by reason of the conflicting evidence of the value of the property in question. He determined to send for the barber in the court house building, and hear his opinion of the value, and thereupon he dispatched the court messenger for Mynheer von Schlizeringberg, the aforesaid barber, to aid him in determining the suit. The messenger accordingly told the Teuton what the judge desired, and after fixing up in his best style he made his way to the court room, and, seeing a vacant seat next the judge (who by-the-way is fond of a joke), the said Teuton ascended the bench and took his seat alongside the court, and became a component part thereof. Judge S——, after taking a sly look at his colleague and the bar, proceeded to hear the witnesses; and the adjunct of the court, taking out his pencil, began figuring up the amount of the damages, and after he had heard the witnesses pronounced judgment: "As I am a parper, and unterstant de case, and dis court knows notings of it, I gif shudgment for de plaintiff tree huntret tollar, and fivf tollar for mineself and de shudge for deciding de case." Of course the "shudgment" was heard amidst roars, which the new judge took as a compliment; he did not find out the real cause until the judge instructed him to go into the witness-box and be sworn.

—

A Distinction With A Difference

In the early days of Iowa, owing to the sparse population and scarcity of better men, it occasionally happened that persons of very ordinary capacity were elected justices of the peace. One of these dignitaries, a certain Squire Blank, of Cedar County, was retained in office by the Democracy for several years, although his intellectual faculties were exceedingly obtuse. Now it so happened that in a certain suit tried before him the defendant, against whom judgment had been rendered, believing that justice had not been done in the premises, took an appeal to the District Court, which at that time was presided over by Judge Tuthill, of Tipton, whose name has already been commemorated in the Drawer. The case was duly reached on the calendar, and a trial *de novo* ordered. A jury was about being impaneled, and among them appeared our friend, the quondam justice of the peace. Upon his name being called the attorney for the appellant objected to him as a juror on the ground that he had both formed and expressed an opinion on the merits of the case, referring the judge to the transcript of the trial below, duly certified by said Blank as J. P.

After looking at the document for a moment the judge, in his usual quiet manner, but with a luminous twinkle of the eye, remarked, "It is true, as appears by the record, that Mr. Blank has *expressed* an opinion, but it does not consequently follow that he has ever *formed* one. The objection is overruled, and Mr. Blank will take his seat in the jury-box."

The point was seen and properly appreciated, not only by the members of the bar, but by all present, who seemed fully to understand the quaint decision.

Leg Pulling

A well-known member of the Westchester bar obtained a verdict for the plaintiff in a negligence case before a certain judge. The lawyer's adversary moved for a new trial, or for a reduction of the verdict, on the ground that there was no evidence of permanent injury, in that the plaintiff had not shown that his injured leg was shorter than it had been before the accident. The motion was promptly denied, and the judge called up the plaintiff's attorney to the bench. He whispered that the point was a nice one, but as the court was satisfied that plaintiff's attorney would pull plaintiff's leg sufficiently in the case, he had disregarded it.

Diamond Cut Diamond

Chief Justice Shea, of the Marine Court of New York, occasionally availed himself of an opportunity to take down those members of the bar who were unmindful of the proprieties. Not long since, two gentlemen who were trying a case before his honor gave each other the lie direct. Judge Shea, after a moment's pause, remarked, in his quiet, bland way, "As no one in court appears to contradict *either* of the gentlemen, let the argument proceed."

Brady's Mot

Judges will on occasion have their little joke. Recently at the General Term, in New York, held by Judges Davis, Brady and Daniels, a lawyer remarked, by the way of illustrating his case:

"Suppose, for example, I borrowed from one of your honors a thousand dollars, and gave this paper as security, could there be any doubt of your right to recover?"

Judge Davis. "But where could we get the money?"

Lawyer. "That's a conundrum: I give it up."

Judge Brady. "There should be no trouble about the money, as we are *sitting in bank.*"

CHAPTER VIII

The Reply that Silences

No Desire to Catch Her

James F. Sweeney of the Suffolk (Massachusetts) bar, is noted for the brightness and aptness of his retorts. "Recently in a case a woman was very refractory under cross-examination, and although the lawyer used all politeness and mildness, sharp and unsatisfactory replies were received. Her meek and humble husband was present in court. Mr. Sweeney tried another innocent question, when the lady responded with vindictive fire flashing from her eyes: 'Mr. Lawyer, you needn't think you can catch me; no, sir, you can't catch me.' With his most pleasing smile Mr. Sweeney responded: 'Madam, I haven't the slightest desire to catch you, and your husband looks to me as if he was sorry he had succeeded.' A ripple of laughter went round the court room, the judge stroked his mustache to hide a smile, and the crier rapped for order."

The Way in Court

A story is told of the late Chief Justice Fuller. He was once counsel for the plaintiff in a certain case, and a Mr. B—— was the defendant. Fuller called a witness and proceeded to examine him.

"I understand," he said, "that you called on the plaintiff, Mr. Smith. Is that so?"

"Yes," replied the man.

"What did he say?" demanded Fuller.

Mr. B—— promptly rose and objected. The conversation could not be admitted as evidence, but Fuller persisted, and Mr. B—— appealed to the judges, who thereupon retired to consider the point. They were absent for nearly half an hour. When they returned they announced that Mr. Fuller might put his question.

"Well what did he say?" asked counsel.

"Please, sir, he wasn't at home," replied the witness, without moving a muscle.

Tit for Tat

After the Hon. Cave Johnson had served his long and brilliant career in Congress, after he had distinguished himself as President Polk's Postmaster-General, after he had resigned with honor the presidency of the Bank of Tennessee, and had retired to the quiet of private life, he once stepped into the office of his nephew, Robert Johnson, then a young lawyer of much promise, and finding the young man engaged in writing with a gold pen, had occasion to remark upon the extravagance of the rising generation.

"Why is it," said he, "that every young man now has his gold pen, while those of my day were content to use their goose-quills?"

"I suppose," replied Robert, in the most innocent manner possible, "it is because there were more *geese* when you were a young man."

When Greek Meets Greek

There once lived in Kentucky a clever gentleman and an excellent lawyer as well, Judge D——, who was intimate with Governor R——, living in an adjacent county. Governor R—— was an old-time Virginia gentleman of stately dignity. The judge was on a visit at the old Governor's house, and it happened that the Governor took him out riding in his buggy, and that in passing along the turnpike they approached a toll-gate. Upon the judge's taking out his purse as if to pay toll the Governor said, in his stately way, "I've been a long time trying to make you a gentleman to little purpose, I see. You must know, sir, that *when a gentleman takes a gentleman out riding, he does not expect him to pay his passage.*" The judge put up his pocketbook and said nothing. After a while they came to a gate on the Governor's place, when the Governor stopped the buggy for the young judge to get out and open the gate; but the judge sat still, and was silent. After a while, still waiting, the Governor said, "Ahem! ahem!" waiting for the judge to move, and then again "Ahem! ahem!" After a good long pause the judge said, "Governor R——, you must know, sir, that *when a gentleman takes a gentleman out to ride, he doesn't expect him to work his passage.*"

Sarcasm From the Bench

The following experience of a Mississippi lawyer was related by himself many years ago. He said:

I was defending a prisoner for horse-stealing, and seeing no other means of defending him, under the circumstances, I set up the plea of insanity. I argued it at length, read many extracts from works of medical jurisprudence, and had the patient attention of the court. The prosecuting attorney did not attempt to reply to my argument or controvert my authorities; I seemed to have things my own way, and whispered to the prisoner that he needn't be uneasy. Then came the judge's charge, in which he reminded the jury that there was no dispute between counsel as to the facts of the case. Indeed, there could not have been, for several witnesses had sworn positively that they saw my client steal the horse. "But," concluded the court, "the plea of insanity has been set up, and I charge you, gentlemen of the jury, that it should receive your very grave and serious deliberation; but I must be allowed to say, gentlemen, that for myself, upon a review of the whole case, I can discover no evidence of insanity on the part of the prisoner, except, perhaps, in the selection of his counsel."

Conveniently Deaf

Many years ago there was a judge in Boston who was more noted for his sound judgment and great knowledge of the law than for his courtesy to counsel or suitor. One day at the opening of a term of his court a large number of gentlemen drawn as jurors begged to be excused from serving. As one after another gave his reasons, a frown began to grow on the judge's face. Another man asked to be let off.

"What for?"

"I cannot hear readily, and am afraid I may not get all the evidence."

"How long have you been deaf?" asked the judge, in a low tone.

"About ten years."

"Can you hear ordinary conversation?—can you hear me now?" said the judge, dropping his voice almost to a whisper.

"Oh, yes, sir, I can hear you."

The judge looked sternly at him a full minute. Then he said: "Mr. Clerk, excuse this man. If he is deaf we don't want him, and if he is a liar we don't want him."

No more excuses were made that day.

Retort That Cost a Lawyer $50

The appointment of Judge Stafford of Vermont to the district bench, to succeed Judge Pritchard, called forth this story from Representative Foster, of that state:

"When Chief Justice Chase, a man of great abilities and marked characteristics, was presiding in one of the county courts of Vermont, an appeal case from a justice's court came up before him so small and contemptible in its origin that he ordered it stricken from the docket. The case was where a turkey had trespassed upon the garden of a neighbor and got shot for his depredations. The owner brought suit to recover damages, and, failing before the justice, had appealed the case. Judge Chase was angry, and when he ordered the case from the docket, said:

"'The lawyer who consented to appeal this case ought to be thrown from the window of the court room. Why didn't he have the case referred to some of the honest neighbors for settlement?'

"'Because, your honor,' retorted the attorney, 'it was our intention not to let honest people have anything to do with it.'

"True, this was a neat retort, but it cost the lawyer just an even $50 for contempt of court."

Preferred the Burglar

The wife of a man accused of house-breaking was in the witness-box, and the prosecuting attorney was conducting a merciless cross-examination.

"Madam, you are the wife of this man?"

"Yes."

"You knew he was a burglar when you married him?"

"Yes."

"How did you come to contract a matrimonial alliance with such a man?"

"Well," said the witness, sarcastically, "I

was getting old, and had to choose between a lawyer and a burglar!"

The cross-examination ended right there.

A Sad Plight

Tudor Jenks, the author of many bits of humorous verse and prose, and of several successful children's books, has always had hard work on first meeting people to get them to accept his name as his own. They have insisted on regarding it as a clever pseudonym. Latterly the matter has grown worse, and he has experienced difficulty in establishing its right to a place in articulate speech.

One day, in front of the Fifth Avenue Hotel, Mr. Jenks was an involuntary witness of a fight between two cab drivers. The men were promptly arrested and Mr. Jenks was hauled away to court with them to tell what he had seen. The police judge was elderly, gruff and short-tempered. Mr. Jenks took the stand.

"What is your name?" asked the lawyer.

"Tudor Jenks."

"Once more, please."

"Tudor Jenks."

Sharp rap from the court, and this explosively:

"Witness will stop making a funny noise and give his name!"

Evaded Company

At a trial in the Court of Common Pleas in Sandusky, Ohio, in 1872, several citizens were subpœnaed to testify as to the character and habits of A—— B——, defendant. Among the number was an ex-probate judge of grave demeanor. The state attorney asked this gentleman if he was acquainted with the defendant, and he replied, "Yes."

"Are you sufficiently acquainted with the defendant to know his general habits?"

"Yes, sir."

"Are they good, or bad?"

"Fair."

"Now, sir, do you before this court and jury testify that you are in the habit of associating with the same kind of company as this defendant?"

"Oh, yes; I associate with all grades of company, *from lawyers up.*"

His Scruples

At certain times, in courts of justice, it has been difficult to obtain men of intelligence and impartiality to act as jurors, especially in capital cases. At a term of the Oyer and Terminer, held in New York, Mr. Justice Davis presiding, this difficulty presented itself. The trial impending was for murder, and the large panel summoned for the purpose was nearly exhausted. The name of an intelligent Hebrew gentleman was called; he took the stand, and was asked the usual questions as to whether he had read the papers and formed an opinion as to the guilt or innocence of the prisoner. He replied that he had not. He was next interrogated as to whether he had conscientious scruples as to hanging in case of conviction for murder. He answered that he had. The District Attorney promptly objected to his being accepted, and the gentleman was about to retire, doubtless gratified at not being compelled to endure the fatigue and anxiety of a prolonged trial, when the counsel for the prisoner said, "Wait a moment, if you please. You say you have scruples in reference to hanging for the crime of murder?"

"I have," was the reply.

"What is the nature of your scruples?"

"*Well, sir, I am strongly and conscientiously in favor of hanging people who commit murder!*"

The prompt, blunt, altogether unexpected as

well as unprecedented answer raised an audible smile throughout the court room, and took judge, counsel, and audience quite by surprise. It was, on the whole, however, thought best—especially for the defense—to let the gentleman depart.

On Pressing Business

The Honorable "Champ" Clark recently told of a case brought up in Missouri in which one of the lawyers engaged tried to serve his client by throwing suspicion on a certain witness during the course of his cross-examination.

The first question put was:

"You admit that you were at the prisoner's home every evening during this period?"

"Yes, sir," replied the witness.

"State whether you and he were interested in any special transaction, such as, for instance, business or otherwise."

"Yes, sir, we were."

"Oh, ho!" exclaimed the wily attorney. "Then you will no doubt be good enough to inform us how and to what extent, also the nature of the business in which you were jointly interested."

"I haven't the least objection in the world," cheerfully answered the obliging witness. "If you want to know—I was courting his daughter!"

A Good Friday Spell

Good Friday is not a day suggestive of mirth, yet it has given birth to one little witticism that lawyers sometimes refer to facetiously on Holy Thursday. It is of the Protestant judge who on the latter day directed the crier, in the usual way, to "adjourn court until to-morrow morning." "What!" exclaimed a holy lawyer, "adjourn until *to-morrow!* Why, your honor, to-morrow will be Good Friday, and the only judge ever known to hold court on that day was Pontius Pilate!" Of course a further adjournment was ordered. This anecdote elicited the statement from a gentleman of prominence on the bench that judicial records furnish no instance of a criminal having been sentenced or executed on Good Friday.

Too Much Display

One of the most common defects of a recently-admitted lawyer is a striving for oratorical display. A successful old practitioner endeavors, on the other hand, to give the jury a heart-to-heart talk.

A story is told of two farmers who were returning home, one of them from jury duty in a neighboring town. "Lawyer Smith is a great orator," said one,—"a perfect Daniel Webster. My, how I hated to decide against him in the three cases he tried!"

"How about Lawyer Jones, who was on the other side?"

"Oh, shucks! why of course he wins all his cases. I heard every one of 'em, and they were the simplest things. He just explained things to the jury. He didn't have to do any hard talking at all. You couldn't help but agree with him."

The Judge, No Doubt, Knew

After his famous farewell dinner at Bangor, a friend approached Chief Justice Peters and in a complimentary way said: "Well, judge, one thing is sure. There'll never be another dinner just like that." The judge looked at the friend with a twinkle in his eye and solemnly said in a whisper: "My dear boy, I'm not so clear that there ever ought to be."

Useless Labor

Some years ago several deputies had a gathering at the home of Sheriff Lane in Gloucester.

While looking about the house, Mr. Lane called the attention of his visitors to an old clock, a great favorite of his. He told his friends of his great attachment to the piece of mechanism, getting quite pathetic at parts of its history, and ending by saying, "And, gentlemen, I have wound up that clock every night for so many years" (mentioning the number). Here an old deputy turned the tide of feeling evoked by the story by saying, "Well, Lane, I always did think that you were a darned old fool! That's an *eight-day clock!*"

An Unimportant Point

In a certain Kansas county, where prohibition was rampant, the grand jury, after having examined sundry citizens without material result, at length cast their net over one Klawback, a moss-grown but shrewd old fellow.

Did Mr. Klawback know of any violations of the prohibitory law? Waal, yes; Mr. Klawback, after raking around his memory, reckoned he did, and after being directed to say on, explained that he himself had purchased a quantity of liquor some two months before from a man in a neighboring hamlet in the same county, which liquor, the speaker earnestly averred, with a reminiscent smack of his lips, was the best that he had had the pleasure of putting into his head for many moons—it had burnt the throat right out of him. The essential facts of his testimony were duly recorded, the indictment triumphantly made out, and the constable sent for to apprehend the purveyor of the vile stuff, when the ingenuous Mr. Klawback bethought himself of something.

"Waal, now, gen'lemen," he drawled, "I don't know as it makes any pertickler difference, but I sorter forgot to tell you that the inickertous scoundrel that sold me that whiskey died early yesterday mornin'."

And So He Sat Down

A certain judge had his patience sorely tried by lawyers who wished to talk and by men who tried to evade jury service. Between hypothetical questions and excuses it seemed as if they never would get to the actual trial of the case. So when the puzzled little German who had been accepted by both sides jumped up, the judge was exasperated.

"Shudge!" cried the German.

"What is it?" demanded the judge.

"I tink I like to go home to my vife," said the German.

"You can't," retorted the judge. "Sit down."

"But, shudge," persisted the German, "I don't tink I make a good shuror."

"You're the best in the box," said the judge. "Sit down."

"But, shudge," continued the little German, "I don't speak goot English."

"You don't have to speak any at all," said the judge. "Sit down."

The little German pointed to the lawyers, to make his last desperate plea.

"Shudge," he said, "I can't make noddings out of what dese fellars say."

It was the judge's chance to get even for many annoyances.

"Neither can any one else," he said. "Sit down."

With a sigh the little German sat down.

What is "Reputation"?

Among the lawyers of one of our large Eastern cities was "Squire G.," as he was commonly called, whose common boast was that never did any witness get the better of him. In defending a man accused of retailing liquor without a license, however, Squire G. met his equal. The principal witness for the prosecution had testified that the defendant's "grocery" had the reputation of being a liquor saloon. In the cross-examination the following colloquy took place:

Squire G. "I understand you to say that this place had the reputation of being a place where liquor was sold?"

Witness. "Yes, sir, so I said."

G. "Was this reputation a general one?"

W. "Yes, sir, it was."

G. "Whom did you ever hear say that it was such a place?"

W. "I do not know that I ever heard any one say so."

G. "Yet you say that it had such a general reputation?"

W. "Yes, sir."

Mr. G. evidently thought that now he had the witness in a tight corner, and leaning back with a complacent smile, he asked, in a triumphant way, "Now be so kind as to tell the jury what you mean by saying a place has the reputation of being a liquor saloon, yet you never heard any one say it was."

"Well, Squire G., I'll illustrate," replied the witness. "I believe you have the reputation of being a smart lawyer, but I will take oath that I never heard any one say you were."

CHAPTER IX

Justices' Justice

An Odd Decision

IN a South Carolina city, not many years ago, a fight occurred on the street between two citizens. One of the belligerents, breaking away from the other, rushed into the middle of the street and picked up a stone, which he threw at his antagonist with great force. The other dodged, and the missile smashed through a plate-glass window in the front of a store. The proprietor ran out hurriedly, and soon had the two men taken before a police magistrate for trial. The case hinged upon who should pay for the broken window. The justice heard a good many witnesses, and when he had taken the testimony of the fighters themselves he pondered for a few moments, and then delivered himself about as follows:

"There is no doubt that a window was broken. Who is to pay for it? There is no doubt that the man who threw the stone had no intention of inflicting any damage on the window. He threw at his antagonist. Had the latter remained still, he would, in all probability, have been struck by the stone, and the window would not have been broken. Now, therefore, in view of the fact that the thrower of the stone had no desire to break the window, and as it was done only when the other man dodged, I declare that the damages for the window are to be charged to the man who would have been struck had he not stepped aside in order to be safe from the stone. The other prisoner is discharged."

Fined Anyway

"I can't convict you on the evidence," said a certain rural justice, "but I'm goin' to fine you $10 for contempt for lookin' like I couldn't!" And he did.

Pure Gallantry

Recently a suit was tried before an Indiana justice of the peace wherein a lady was plaintiff, and a bank the defendant. The evidence showed conclusively that the fair plaintiff had no right to recover; of this no one could have the "shadow of a doubt." Her learned counsel knew well that unless he could get the sympathy of the "squire," his client would have a "lost cause." He therefore labored hard in applying the "sympathetic process." He gushed with eloquence of great warmth in referring to his client's rights, until finally great tears came trickling down his cheeks, at the sight of which the justice (who was a very tender-hearted individual) was also moved to tears. This satisfied the attorney that the sympathy of the court was in behalf of the lady, and he closed his argument by saying, "It does my heart good to believe that this honorable court, in the exercise of a sound discretion, will not allow the rights of a pure and noble lady to be trampled beneath the cloven feet of a soulless corporation"; and took his seat, as confident that he would get a judgment as ever poor Miss Flite was.

Thereupon the squire rendered the following comprehensive and satisfactory decision. He said: "The plaintiff in this case is a woman, and her counsel has for the last hour touched the sympathy of the court in her behalf, and I am glad of it; but I think, under the law, that justice is on the side of the bank. I therefore will find in favor of the bank, and let *the record show that Mrs. ——— has the full sympathy of the court.*"

The Sentence of the Court

Former Senator Mason, of Illinois, was waiting for a train in one of the villages near Chicago. To pass the time away he went into the office of the local justice of the peace. The justice was an old fellow, good-natured, and with little knowledge of the law.

A young man was brought in charged with disturbing a religious meeting. Evidence was presented to show that he did disturb the meeting. After the evidence was in, the young man told the justice he was very sorry, that he would never do it again and begged to be let off.

The justice of the peace wiped his spectacles and cleared his throat. "Boy," he said, "I know your father and your mother. They have been my lifelong friends. I have known you since you were a baby, but—but ——" The old man broke down and cried. When he had recovered himself he continued: "But justice is blind. I sentence you to two years in the penitentiary."

Senator Mason then arose and said he had no interest in the case, but he did not want the court to make an error. He told the justice he had no jurisdiction, that he could not impose such a sentence.

"No juris what?" asked the old man between sobs.

Mason explained what he meant. "Well," said the old justice, smiling broadly, "I'm glad I haven't. Johnny, you can go. Skedaddle!"

A New Jersey Solomon

Magistrate Jermon, a Philadelphia legal light, once spent a summer in a little town in South Jersey and made the acquaintance of a justice of the peace who held more offices than Pooh Bah himself. "He was," says Jermon, "a notary public, a storekeeper, superintendent of the Sunday-school, a lay preacher, postmaster, coroner, a farmer and a few more things that I can't recall now. He was a shrewd old fellow, as a decision in a case that I heard will go to show. Two farmers had a dispute about the ownership of some poultry, and each pleaded his own case. Each side had an equal number of witnesses and there was some tall swearing done all around. If I had been sitting on the case I should have given it up as a bad job, or sent it to court for trial. But that's just what he didn't do.

"I forgot to state that in addition to all his other functions he was his own constable. The hens were in court in a coop and he ordered that the constable should take the coop to the roadway opposite the farms of the litigants and turn the creatures loose. And he did the job himself and got his fee for doing it. The hens settled the case by going directly to one of the farms, and the justice declared that they knew their way home, and gave judgment accordingly."

Justice Barnard's Way

Among the anecdotes told about the late Justice Barnard, of Poughkeepsie, is the following incident which occurred some years ago:

Judge Augustus Schoonmaker of Kingston noticed a motion before Justice Barnard in a case in which Judge F. L. Westbrook was attorney on the other side. Both attorneys were well acquainted with Justice Barnard.

Westbrook took an early train. When he arrived in Poughkeepsie he received a telegram from Schoonmaker saying that he had missed the train and would be down later.

He went to Justice Barnard's court room and sat down. By and by the court ran out of business, and Justice Barnard inquired:

"Fred, what do you want?"

Judge Westbrook explained that he was there to defend a motion to be made by Judge Schoonmaker, that Schoonmaker had missed the train, and that he was expecting him every minute, and that he did not wish to take his default.

In about ten minutes Justice Barnard began to grow restless and said to Judge Westbrook:

"Fred, let me see your papers."

Judge Westbrook handed over his papers, which, of course, contained a copy of the notice of motion, with affidavits on both sides. Justice Barnard read them through, and said:

"Motion denied, $10 costs to abide the event."

"But what shall I tell Judge Schoonmaker?" stammered Westbrook.

"Oh, tell him the motion is denied, and he can go back home," was the answer.

Arbitrary Procedure

It's all in the way in which things are stated, thinks a Dakota lawyer, who is of opinion that the following way of putting it may be interesting to lawyers and judges in the East. A case was on trial at Sioux Falls before a justice of the peace. The suit was in replevin, and the attorney for the defendant made a logical argument tending to show the insufficiency of the affidavit for replevin. The justice, after casting his eyes thoughtfully to the ceiling for a moment, decided the point thus: "Gentlemen, after serious reflection upon this matter, I can't see that this affidavit *cuts any particular figure* in this case *just at this stage of the game.* Motion denied. Call in your witnesses."

His Costs

In Georgia a justice of the peace receives no salary, but is dependent solely upon "costs" for the emoluments of office. Consequently it is a position not sought by the highest order of talent, and instances of "justices' justice" are not of such rare occurrence as might be desired. The following is vouched for as a true story:

Mr. M——, a farmer living near a middle Georgia town, one day found an estray cow in his pasture. Shortly afterward a negro called, and, claiming the cow, was told that if he would produce satisfactory proof of ownership he might take her. Next to watermelons and 'possums the Georgia negro is fondest of a lawsuit; to sue and be sued gives him a realizing sense of the dignity of citizenship. Here was an opportunity not to be lost, and so, instead of satisfying M—— that the cow really belonged to him, which he easily could have done, the negro consulted a young attorney in town, and was advised to take out a possessory warrant for the animal. This was accordingly done, and in due time the case came on for trial before the local magistrate. M—— came into court, disclaimed ownership or right of possession, and turned the cow over to the bailiff to be disposed of as the court should direct.

After a lengthy argument by the "counsel for the plaintiff" (the negro requires that his physician shall administer allopathic doses), the court announced that as the case was one deserving of careful consideration he would reserve his decision until ten o'clock the following morning.

Promptly at the appointed hour the negro, accompanied by his counsel and a number of interested spectators, entered the court room. The magistrate ascended the split-bottomed seat of justice, adjusted his spectacles, arranged the code and form books in order on his table, and delivered *ex cathedra* the following opinion:

"This case involves a p'int of consider'ble importance, 'bout which the Court don't find nothin' laid down in the Code. Ther' ain't no doubt 'bout the cow belongin' to the nigger, and the Court decides that p'int in his favor. But who's li'ble for the costs? Accordin' to law the party losin' the case must pay the costs. Who air the parties to this suit? In ev'ry case ther' must be two parties—a plaintiff and a defendant. Now it's clare the nigger's the plaintiff, but who's the defendant? Mr. M—— can't be the defendant, because he didn't claim the cow, and didn't make no defense to this suit. This leaves the nigger and the cow as the only rale parties befo' the Court, *and the nigger bein' the plaintiff, the cow must be the defendant.* The plaintiff havin' won the case, the defendant is li'ble for the costs. Mr. Bailiff, I direct you to *hold the cow 'til the costs air paid.*"

As The Judge Understood It

A lawyer, addressing a jury in a Billville justice court, quoted, in defense of his client—"Honi soit qui mal y pense," whereupon the justice, striking the desk a thundering blow with his fist, shouted:

"You'll never do it, sir—not in this court!"

"Do what, your honor?" asked the surprised attorney.

"Hit 'em a swat an' pitch 'em over the fence, sir!" replied the justice.

CHAPTER X

Strained Situations

Her Age

An aged woman by the name of Samantha Skaggs, who for many years had resided near Ripley, Illinois, and was known by her numerous descendants and all the people of the countryside as Grandmother Skaggs, was compelled to go to court to testify as a witness in a lawsuit over a disputed will.

"Mrs Skaggs," said the attorney for the defense, in cross-examining her, "may I ask how old you are?"

"Do I have to tell that, judge?" she said, appealing to the court.

"Why, yes, madam," replied the judge. "It's a proper question, and at your time of life you surely need not be sensitive about your age."

"Well," she answered, "I'm ninety-seven."

But she told it with evident embarrassment and reluctance.

She knew that everybody in the neighborhood believed her to be one hundred.

A Judicial Request

On one occasion Sir Matthew Bigbee, of the Supreme Court of British Columbia, presided at a trial where a man was before the court on a charge of sand-bagging. The evidence was almost conclusive against the prisoner, but, much to every one's surprise, the jury brought in a verdict of "Not guilty."

Sir Matthew was both surprised and disgusted, and when discharging the prisoner remarked: "Prisoner, you are discharged. Now if you wish to oblige me particularly you will go to work at once and sand-bag that jury."

Canadian Justice

The following story comes from one of the members of the Montreal (Canada) bar, who was actually engaged as counsel in the trial:

"The prosecution was for nuisance, and was brought nominally by her Majesty against the owners of one of the largest ironworks in that city. The residents in the neighborhood had subscribed funds and retained counsel, a true bill was found, and the case proceeded before the Court of Queen's Bench (crown side). The usual testimony was adduced. Householders told dreadful tales of the damage done to property by the immense quantity of smoke emitted from the low chimneys of the defendants' furnaces; housewives testified that their washing was constantly spoiled when hung out to dry in their yards or on their roofs; and medical men swore to the deleterious effects of the smoke on the public health. Toward the conclusion of the case we put a gentleman from the Emerald Isle on the stand. He owned a small property close to the rolling-mills, and thus proceeded: 'Yer anner and gintlemin av the jury, oi will tell me shtory in me own way. Oi live nixt door to a party be the name av Grogan—Jerry Grogan, yer anner—a dacint married man wid a woife and four shlips av bhoys. Wan day whin the chimneys av the rollin'-mills was puffin' out shmoke like the divil, oi hears a terrible row goin' an in Jerry Grogan's house, shoutin' and shcreamin' and yellin'. Oi goes up to the door, and sez oi, "Let me in." "Come in, for God's sake," sez Mrs. Grogan; "Jerry is killin' me," sez she. And in oi goes, and sees Jerry wallupin' the woife. "Jerry," sez oi, "what are ye batin' the woife for?" sez oi. Sez Jerry to me, sez he, "She's got niggers in the house," sez he. "Niggers!" sez oi. "Yes," sez he. "Where is the niggers?" sez oi. "In the room beyant," sez Jerry. And so oi goes into the room beyant, and sings out to Jerry, "Jerry, ye're a fool," sez oi. "What for?" sez he. "Beca'se," sez oi, "thim's no niggers," sez oi. "Well, what the divil are they?" sez he. "Jerry," sez oi, "ye're mad," sez oi. *And, yer anner and gintlemin av the jury, thim niggers was Jerry's own children, begrimed by the shmoke from the defindants' facthory chimneys.'"*

The Dog Knew

A lawyer in central New York tells this story at his own expense about one of his first cases.

"My client sued a neighbor for the alleged killing of a favorite dog. The proof consisted in the mysterious disappearance of the animal, and the possession of a dog's skin by the defendant, which, after considerable argument, was brought into court in evidence. It was marked in a singular manner, and was positively identified, with many tears, by the plaintiff's wife and daughter as the undoubted integument of the deceased Bose. In summing up to the jury, I was in the midst of a highly-colored picture of the virtues of the deceased, and of the love of the children for their four-footed friend, when I was interrupted by a slight disturbance in the crowd near the door of the little schoolhouse which served as court-house. Looking around, I saw my client's youngest son, a tow-headed urchin of twelve, coming forward with a dog whose skin was the exact counterpart of the one put in evidence. The dog wagged his tail with good-natured composure, and the boy cried, in his childish treble, 'Paw, Bose has come home.' I gathered up my law books and retreated, and I have never had perfect confidence in circumstantial evidence since."

A Busy Time

A certain judge, somewhat famed for the prolixity and subtlety of his reasoning, looked at a confused and bewildered witness, while his face took on the most benign expression as he endeavored to straighten out the question which had been propounded by counsel.

"Now, my good woman," he said, cheerfully and reassuringly, "you have only to answer in the fewest possible words these simple queries: Whether when you were crossing the street with the baby on your arm, and the stage was coming down on the right, and the cab on the left, and the brougham was trying to pass the stage, you saw the plaintiff between the brougham and the cab, or the brougham and the stage, whether he seemed in haste, and which one of the three cabs coming from the other direction he appeared to you to be hailing?"

The now thoroughly bewildered witness wiped her spectacles and meekly made answer:

"Yes, your honor!"

A Fire-Eating Judge

There was a Judge Henry, Chief Justice of Missouri. He was a clean, brave gentleman of that bulldog kind of heart that is at once tender and ferocious. In deciding a certain case Judge Henry described an individual, who until then had thought highly of himself, as a thief and scoundrel. The next afternoon Judge Henry was strutting up the walk to the State House. The ill-used one met him, a six-shooter in his hand and his hand under the cloak of his coat.

"You are circulating rumors about me, Judge Henry!" said the ill-used one.

"No rumors, sir!" retorted Judge Henry. "I said you were a thief and scoundrel, sir!"

"Bang!" went the gun.

The bullet tore along Judge Henry's forearm, and then broke two of his ribs. Judge Henry shattered his cane upon the other's head, felling him. Seeing that the enemy did not get up, Judge Henry continued his strut to the State

House, and went into the office of Governor Crittenden.

"Heavens, judge! what's the matter?" exclaimed the governor.

"That thief and scoundrel whom I characterized has shot me," said Judge Henry.

"Here!" said the governor, "let me send for a doctor."

"No," returned Judge Henry, "you send for a telegraph boy and wire Mrs. Henry that I'm not hurt. This story will be in Kansas City in ten minutes, and I don't propose to have her frightened with it."

Blood and Iron

"Sir!" returned Judge Henry with one of his customary frowns, "sir, not alone could I do justice to an enemy in my court, but I could do justice to a friend in my court. It wouldn't hurt a man in my court, sir, to have been my friend."

Adam vs. Adam

Adam Riddle and Adam Hodge, members of the Cincinnati bar, were on one occasion engaged on opposite sides in a land case, and in their legal discussions were both very learned and astute. They succeeded, both of them, in bothering the court, each other, and themselves in their attempted analysis of the intricate legal questions and points involved in the obdurate land case. At last Brother Hodge, in total despair of appreciation of the nice points of his adversary, exclaimed, "My brother opponent, Adam Riddle, I must be allowed to say, in the curious and cumbersome points which he has raised, is *a dam Riddle* to me, begging the indulgence of the court for apparent profanity." Whereupon Brother Riddle, immediately interrupting, arose and said, "I excuse the brother for not understanding me and my law points; but if the court will permit, I pronounce him, in his land law points, *a dam Hodge-podge*, sir." Both were equally indulged, as being equally pointed.

Importance of Tact

An excellent case was once lost purely and simply because of want of tact. An individual possessing fiery red hair happened to be run down at a street crossing. As luck would have it, the horse was a white one. The defendant's counsel imagined that here was a good opportunity and proceeded to make a number of witty remarks relative to red hair and white horses. Everybody laughed. They couldn't help it.

Unfortunately, however, there happened to be a man on the jury whose hair was a very dark shade of auburn, and he was absurdly sensitive on the point. The method by which that man, who was of an exceedingly stubborn nature, brought the rest of the jury around to a verdict for the plaintiff is a mystery, but he did it.

Start of an Iowa Lawyer

An Iowa practitioner tells the following story of his first months of practice.

He went to a small country town, and secured an office room in front of which was placed the usual sign. Then he sat down and waited for his clients to appear, all the while feeling very much the dignity of his position. The day passed, and no one called, and another, and another, until weeks went by and still there had been no client.

One morning, however, he was at the station to attend upon the arrival of the daily accommodation train, quite an important function of the town, when a handsome, well-dressed young lady appeared and inquired:

""Is this Mr. Smith?"

At once the feeling of importance returned, and in his blandest tones he replied, scenting a case of some value:

"It is, madam. What can I do for you?"

Judge of his chagrin upon receiving the following answer:

"Can you tell me how much it will cost to send a sow and pigs down to the next station?"

The widest stretch of imagination could not torture the information asked for into "professional services."

Splitting the Difference

In a jury trial in a small town not many miles from civilization, the rural gentlemen into whose hands the fate of the plaintiff and defendant was placed were so stubbornly divided that they were some twenty odd hours in reaching a verdict. As they left the court, after having rendered the verdict, one of them was asked by a friend what the trouble was.

"Waal," he said, "six on 'em wanted to give the plaintiff $4,000, and six on 'em wanted to give him $3,000, so we split the difference an' gave him $500."

Acted According to Law

A certain New York lawyer had succeeded in securing for a friend of his, after considerable exertion, a place as tax assessor.

Not long after the friend had begun his duties

in his new place the lawyer was surprised and grieved to receive a notice that under "personal property" he was taxed twenty-four dollars as the possessor of one goat.

He called on his friend, the new assessor, and asked for an explanation, accusing him of ingratitude.

"But I couldn't do less than obey the specific details of the law," protested the new official. "Look,—here's what it says," and he read from his papers:

"For all property bounding or abutting on the highway, twelve dollars per front foot!"

Tender and True

Squire Benson, a country justice, was often consulted in cases of family jars resulting from the storm and stress of time or temper, and he derived no little amusement from the tales told in his private office.

"Is it true that you threw something at Mike that caused the swelling over his eye?" the squire inquired of a little wiry Irishwoman who appeared one day, sobbing as if her heart would break.

"Yis, sor, I did!" said the woman catching her breath, "but I niver wint to hurt him, an' well he knows it! We'd jist come home from me cousin's weddin', an' I was feelin' kinder soft to Mike, an' I up an' axed him if he loved me as much as he did the day we was merried ; an'—an',—yer anner, he was so slow answerin' me that I up wid the mop an' flung it at him ! If we poor wimmen don't have love our hearts jist breaks inside uv us ! "

The Best Advice

The following story is told of a well-known advocate. When General Beck was a young lawyer a man was arraigned for murder and had no counsel.

" Mr. Beck," said the presiding judge, " take the prisoner into that room at the rear of the court, hear his story, and give him the best advice you can."

Accordingly Beck disappeared with the prisoner, and in half an hour's time returned into court,—alone.

" Where is the prisoner ? " asked the judge.

" Well," replied Beck, slowly, " I heard his story, and then I gave him the best advice I could. I said: 'Prisoner, if I were you, I'd get out of that window and make tracks.' He slid down the water pipe, and the last I saw of him he was getting over a stone fence half a mile away ! "

A Bad Fix

In a Western state, whose laws provide for a jury of six in suits before justices of the peace, a German was elected to that high and honorable office. The old gentleman was naturally smart, and being prosperous, was somewhat of an oracle in the neighborhood; but law was a thing he knew as little about as the most of his predecessors and successors of the J. P. genus.

When his first case came on he listened with reasonable attention to the evidence, but with wrapt interest to the arguments of counsel for both plaintiff and defendant.

When the arguments were closed he appeared very ill at ease, and not until reminded that it was his duty to charge the jury did he offer any suggestion touching the case in hand. But he came up to the situation that confronted him like a man and a judge.

"Shendlemens of der shury," he said, "as dis ist mein first oxberience in sharging a shury, I hartly knows vat do say do you. But as eet ist mein tuty to sharge you somedings I vill do der pest vat I knows how.

"Eff you peleeves all vat der lawyer for der blaintiff haf saidt den I sharge you dot eet iss your tuty to find your ferdict for de blaintiff, and assess hees tamages as you dink righdt, not do oxzeet five huntret tollars und der costs, vich you moost nod vorged.

"But eef, on der odder hant, you peleeves all vat der tefendant's lawyer haf said, den eet iss your tuty to find for der tefendant. In dot case you vill shust do id, und say noddings apout id, oxepding der costs, vich you moost not vorged.

"But, shendlemens, if on der odder hant, you are like me apout dis matter, un dondt peleeve a tamt vort vat eider one off dem haf saidt, den I dondt know vot in der hell you are going do to."

A Reversal of Conditions

An able but impractical lawyer at the Kansas City bar retired from political office not long ago, taking with him the confirmed habit of poker playing in lieu of the excellent law practice lost to him while holding political office. His sense of humor, however, was in no wise dulled thereby.

Dropping in one day to visit a fellow lawyer with little less leisure than himself he greeted him with the usual question about business affairs. "Poor with me, very poor," was the reply; "and every cent, in fact, that I do make in the practice of law I lose playing poker, it seems."

"Well, same condition here, old fellow," was the response; "only—every cent I make playing poker I lose practicing law."

Bill Nye's Dog Case

When Bill Nye first left home for the West, "bidding his parents a kind, even affectionate, farewell," and telling them "ever to remember the good example he had set them since the hour of his birth," it was with the expectation of practicing law rather than of embarking in the newspaper business. He had been admitted to the bar, "under cover of darkness," again to quote his own words, and Laramie, Wyoming, seemed to offer a promising field. He hired an office about a block from the livery stable over which later he carried on his journalistic labors, where one "went up two flights of stairs or twisted the tail of the white mule and took the elevator," according to choice.

In the law Nye got on indifferently, though he took it very seriously, his humorous tendency being at that time either unsuspected by himself or rigidly suppressed. One of his first cases called him to the neighboring town of Big Stranger in defense of a Scandinavian named Axelson, whose dog, it was alleged, had bit the plaintiff.

Nye thought it best to ascertain the exact status of the case from his client, so he said:

"Now, Mr. Axelson, tell me about this dog of yours—did he probably bite the man?"

"No," answered the Scandinavian with a jerk of the head which threatened to dislocate his neck. "He bees goot dog, yentle yust like kittens. Bite nottings."

"Then I think we have a clear case," said Nye. "We will introduce evidence to show the dog's good character. Is he a large dog?"

"Yust a meedle-size dog. Not so small like des little dogs what goes ki-yi-yi! Not so big like des large dogs what goes boom-boom-boop! Ay tank mebby he bees a sheep-dog."

"Good," commented Nye. "Sheep-dogs are always gentle, like their charges. He never bit this man. We shall win the case."

When the trial came on considerable difficulty was experienced in getting a jury, since the plaintiff's attorney objected to every man who owned a dog, and Nye promptly challenged every man who was not provided with such an appendage. Finally a working agreement was hit on and twelve men selected who had been dog owners at some time in their lives but were not at the moment in possession of any specimens. Evidence was then introduced. Nye depended chiefly on his client's neighbors, most of them honest Scandinavians like himself, who swore to the mild disposition and generally pacific character of the dog. His ways, it appeared, were ways of pleasantness, and his paths those of peace.

But it remained for Nye himself in his summing up to praise and glorify that dog above all dogs—to beatify him among canines. He had about reached his peroration. "What, gentlemen of the jury," he cried, "shall we say of men who come into this court and try to traduce this gentle creature? What must we think of men who will attempt to poison the minds of twelve upright gentlemen against a poor, dumb, defenseless beast? Gentlemen, you have heard what the honest neighbors of my client have had to say about that dog. You know it is true, but you shall have further evidence, that of your own senses. I understand that the harmless creature is outside. Mr. Axelson," he added, turning to the defendant, "fetch in Fido! Let these twelve intelligent men form their own opinion of him. Seeing is believing. Remember, gentlemen, this is a sheep-dog, trusted associate of lambs! What, gentlemen, says the poet? What—what," he stammered, not having, in fact, the least notion what the poet said. "What says the poet?" he went on resolutely, inwardly praying that his client would appear and save the day. "What—ah, I have it:

> "'My name is Norval; on the Grampian Hills
> My father feeds his flocks.'

Feeds his flocks, gentlemen. Note those flocks. And what sort of a dog did Norval have? One like my client's—one such as stands before you," he added, relieved, a relief which the next moment was tempered with consternation as he saw that the creature was of sinister aspect and about the size of a yearling calf. "You see, gentlemen, you see——" The gentlemen did see. As he spoke the dog, without a sound, sprang forward and grabbed the foreman of the jury by the leg. Instantly all was uproar. The jury mounted chairs, the judge rapped for order and the sheriff reached for his weapons. "What, gentlemen, says the poet?" roared Nye, hoping for another inspiration, but the judge only rapped the louder. Finally the defendant succeeded in pulling the dog off. "What is the jury's verdict?" asked the judge. "We find for the plaintiff," shouted the foreman, and there was no dissenting voice. "Gentlemen," said Nye as he gathered up his law books, "never mind what the poet said. Whatever it was it wasn't strong enough."

CHAPTER XI

Outside the Court Room

His Platform

SOME years ago the late Chief Justice Chase was traveling in the West on circuit. Already his fame as a jurist had gone abroad, and everywhere he went he received many attentions. On a train between Columbus and Cincinnati the judge was one day a passenger, and while the train stopped at the station in Xenia the townspeople, hearing that Chase was aboard, crowded round the train, demanding a speech. Chase consented and went to the rear platform.

Among other things he said was that his platform was to stand by the old flag, which sentiment did not please all of the audience, for one man, pointing to the notice on the car door behind Judge Chase, repeated:

"It is dangerous to stand on the platform!"

"Ah, yes," said the old lawyer, "but it is much more dangerous to have no platform to stand on!"

It Never Rose Above One Story

Chief Justice Story attended a public dinner in Boston at which Edward Everett was present. Desiring to pay a delicate compliment to the latter, the learned judge proposed as a volunteer toast:

"Fame follows merit where Everett goes."

The brilliant scholar arose and responded:

"To whatever heights judicial learning may attain in this country, it will never get above one Story."

Settled Out of Court

For two years George W. Irvin, of Butte City, filled the position of mineral land commissioner for Montana at the national capital. Before Mr. Irvin held this office he had sat on the bench as police magistrate. It was in the days when Butte was in truth all that is implied in the term "mining camp," and physical prowess was as essential to the enforcement of the statutes and ordinances as were the authority and dignity conferred by the ermine. An entry in the police-court docket of the days of Judge Irvin partly tells its own story.

"George Morton. Charge, drunk and disorderly. Arraigned. Pleaded not guilty. Testimony of Officer Dugan heard. Whereupon court adjudged defendant guilty. At this point defendant arose and announced that he would lick the court at any point in the road. Whereupon court suspended sentence, and announced a recess for fifteen minutes, and a trip to the lot in the rear of the court-room."

There the entry stops, and the inference is the defendant made good his assertion.

An Apt Retort

A story is told at the expense of Joseph Choate, the great lawyer, now ambassador to the Court of St. James. On a very important case, Edward Lauterbach, an eminent Jewish attorney, was associated with him. They won their case and when it came to deciding upon the fee, Mr. Choate, the Christian, asked Mr. Lauterbach, the Jew, what he thought they ought to charge. Mr. Lauterbach said he thought $5,000 would be a fair charge. Mr. Choate replied that it shouldn't be less than $15,000. Said Mr. Lauterbach: "Almost thou persuadest me to be a Christian."

"Git Out and Walk!"

There is a law in Kentucky popularly known as the "Jim Crow Coach Law." By this act colored citizens and plain, or white, citizens must not occupy the same compartment in any coach on any line of railway within the state. In April, 1896, a white man, being a sheriff, had to escort three colored convicts to a penitentiary. The sheriff and his charges boarded a train, and were seated in the "Jim Crow" compartment. In that compartment were a dozen Afro-Americans, blameless before the law. They objected to the presence of a white man in their compartment.

"The Sep'rate Coach Act say no white man shall ride in any compa'tment reserved for cullud citizens," said a black preacher.

"Ain't no question 'bout that," assented a yellow book-agent.

The conductor was called, and a committee of three expounded the law and insisted upon the rights thereby secured to colored citizens. The sheriff argued from the executive exigencies of the occasion.

"I ain't a-goin' to leave them prisoners out o' my sight," he said.

But the conductor, the supreme authority upon a train *in transitu*, decided that the sheriff must get out of the "Jim Crow" compartment, but he might take his three prisoners with him, if he chose, which he did choose. In the smoker, a white folks' compartment, the appearance of the three negro criminals aroused angry feelings.

"Here, captain," shouted a tobacco-cropper, "we can't have no niggers in this compartment." The sheriff rose to make an explanation.

"Gentlemen, I've got to take these here colored convicts to Eddyville. Now, if I can't go in the Jim Crow because I'm white, and the prisoners can't stay in here, bein' niggers, I want you, gentlemen, to tell me how in thunder I'm to deliver my prisoners 'co'din' to my instructions?"

"Git out and walk," was the unanimous verdict, expressed vociferously, and without a second's hesitation.

Meanwhile the train had gone a matter of ten miles from its starting-point. Nevertheless, the sheriff and his prisoners had to get off at a small wayside station, where the pied combination waited some hours before a freight train came along and hospitably received them into its caboose.

Post-Prandial

"Judge Goodliven just went down the street. I thought you said he was attending a big banquet to him this evening."

"Not at all. I saw him coming out of Del's and I merely remarked there was a big dinner in his honor this evening."

Webster Kept It

Many years ago one of the Boston insurance companies had an important case coming on, involving a large sum of money, and the solicitor of the company thought it advisable that Daniel Webster should be retained. The president of the company coincided, and handing him a check for one thousand dollars requested him to call upon Mr. Webster and secure his services. He did so, paying him the money; but it happened that the case was amicably settled. Some time afterward, at the suggestion of the president, Mr. ——— called upon Mr. Webster to inform him that the case would not come to trial, and that the retaining fee should properly be returned to the company. Mr. Webster was amazed. Turning round to Mr. ———, he said: "You are a lawyer, Mr. ———, and know, or certainly ought to know, the meaning of *retainer*. It comes from the Latin retineo—retineo, retinere, retenti, retentum; which means to retain—to retain; and I mean to retain it!"

A Literal Scholar

Prof. Ernest Huffcut, of the Cornell Law School, told an amusing story not long ago of a freshman who was called from the way of knowledge before his year was out.

The students had been answering questions in moot-court, and the subject under discussion was a cow which had been killed by a railway-train. Each student was required to fill out a paper on the case.

"This brilliant youth," said Professor Huffcut, "wrote with all seriousness after 'Disposition of the Carcass': 'Mild and Gentle.'"

Decided Out of Court

In the early days of Judge R——d on the bench of the Sixteenth Judicial District of California, a case came before him wherein the people were plaintiff. As it became necessary to get a change of venue to another county, where a jury could be obtained qualified according to law—by entire ignorance (of the case)—to try the case, the district attorney, a young and promising lawyer, advocated sending it to Amador County, while Judge Marshall, the attorney for the defense, was an equally strong advocate for El Dorado County. Judge R——d, after patiently listening to their seemingly interminable arguments, jokingly suggested that the attorneys should retire and play a game of cribbage, twice around the board, to decide the question. Both attorneys considered themselves experts at this game, and no sooner was the suggestion made than the district attorney sang out, "I'll do it"; whereupon Judge Marshall, equally excited, sang out, "And I'll do it." They immediately retired from the court room, while other business in the court proceeded, and were gone about fifteen minutes, when they returned. The judge thereupon put the question, "Gentlemen, have you agreed to which county your case shall be sent?"

Judge Marshall then arose, in his ponderous, dignified way, and replied, with a broad grin extending from ear to ear, "May it please your honor, you may send it to Amador."

The court was convulsed with laughter. The district attorney had beaten by two points in the game.

A Client's Candor

Here is a story told by one of our women lawyers:

"I told my client to tell me everything just as it had occurred,—to hold back nothing; and then, being perfectly familiar with all the facts,

I might be able to help him. After the story had come to an end I asked him if that were all?"

"Everything,—'cept where I hid th' money!" was the perfectly frank answer.

His Last Offense

Judge D——, of the Circuit Court of the United States for the ——— Circuit, gives the following incident of his experience with a "moonshiner." "I was *en route* to C——, at which place a term of the court commenced next day. At each station, as the train neared C——, the coaches began to fill with a motley crew of deputy-marshals, prisoners, witnesses, and litigants. And finally a butternut jeans specimen dropped into my seat, with, 'I s'pose thar's rume enough fur both orn us, strenger?' I found him communicative, and a few general observations set his tongue agoing. 'Yas, I'm gwine down to C—— to 'tend co't; the gran' jurur hev indicted me for 'stillin'. Well, I've bin thar berfore, but they hain't nuver got me yit. The fax is, ole Jedge F——, which ar' the deestrick jedge, they call 'im, he kinder seems to know our folks, an' sorter ornderstan's this here enturnle revunnue business, an' how them marshuls works it fur fees. But they tells me he's tuck sick, an' hev writ fur an ole jedge named D—— to set fur 'im, who, they sez, is long ords the wust ov the lot. Thet he helt a co't up at R—— wunst, an' carri'd orn ridicklous; thet he wus co't, jurur, an' lawyer, an' mout as well er bin witness. Bob P—— he wus a-tellin' ov it to er crowd at Payne's ole grocery. Ole Lawyer M——, he went down thar to plead fur Bob fur retailen; he wus a good jedge of law, allus so cornsidered, an' er reg'lar ole 'coon dorg before the County Co't, an' sorter run things dar to suit hisself. You could er hearn him open orn a still day cle'r out to Drunkards' Spring, an' thet's a good haft a mile from the co't-house. But Bob sed he didn't stan' no mo' showin' berfore old Jedge D—— then a bobtail bull in fly-time. He sorter jawed back at the jedge fur a whet, an' talked vig'rous 'bout the Decklerashun ov Enderpenjunce, an' the bill ov rights, an' the Constatushun, an' the resulushuns of '98–9. But it didn't make no mo' empresshun orn thet durn, 'segneficant ole jedge then er pourin' water orn a duck's back. He jest sot right down orn Lawyer M——, he did, an' rar'd hisself back in his cha'r, an' sed he werrent a-persidin' at no flag raisen, Fo'th of July doens, nor nuthen ov the sort. An' he 'lowed thet Lawyer M—— didn't know no law, an' didn't hev no everdence. An' he jest tuck his pen, he did, an' he writ out a verdick, an' tole the jurur to assign it; an' the fust thing Bob knowed he war in jail. He sed it war the quickest thing thet he ever seen in his life. Whew! they say he's a plum' sight, an' pow'ful fond er whiskey too, an' I don't ornderstan' why he should be so rantank'rous over them as makes it. Ef haft they say 'bout his drotted meanniss is so, I shouldn't wonder ef he didn't git the whold kit an' bilen orn us this load. The fax is, I'm a gitten tired ov the business, enyhow; it's too dad-fetched unsartin; an' arter feein' the offucers, hiren lawyers, treatin' witnusses, an' payen travullin' expensis a'tendin' ov co't, thar ain't no big chance ov profit in it, no way. Which I tole the ole 'oman. I sez, ef I ken manidge to git cle'r this go-round, I'm a-gwine to close out an' quit the business. Strenger, whar ar' you gwine?'

"I replied that I, too, was on my way to C—— to attend court; and he continued, 'You don't know ole D——, I s'pose?'

"'Yes; I've seen him.'

"'Wal, strenger, ef you kin bring eny enfluunce to b'ar orn 'im, an' kin git me outen this here scrape, I'll fee you hansum.'

"After learning his name, I told him to be

in the court-room next day promptly at ten o'clock. As I took my seat on the bench, the first object that caught my eye was my fellow traveler, leaning over the back railing of the bar. The recognition was mutual. His lower jaw relaxed and dropped until it seemed to hang loose on its hinges, and there was a mingled expression of astonishment and horror on his countenance.

"'Clerk,' said I, 'is there a case of the United States *versus* ——— for illicit distilling on the docket?'

"'Yes, your honor,' said the clerk.

"'*Dismiss it*,' said I.

"It was some little time before he seemed to take in the situation. When he did, he cast a timid, sheepish glance at me, and disappeared in the crowd. I think he kept his word, and went out of the business; at least, I never heard of his name on docket again."

CHAPTER XII

Where Ignorance Is Bliss

In An Indiana Court

"I MET a colored man in the corridor a while ago," said Judge McMaster of the Indianapolis Superior Court. "He was looking for the trial room in which he was to appear as a witness.

"'What sort of case is it?' I asked him.

"'It's one ob dem petty lossity cases!' he answered."

Compact and Lucid

The Hon. Tim Tarsney, Solicitor of the City of Detroit, tells the story of an old Irishman who was nominated for the post of justice of the peace. He owed the distinction rather to his natural gifts than to his learning or judicial ability.

However, the old man was elected, much to his own surprise, and on election night at a certain resort the "boys" called on him for a speech. This is a verbatim report thereof:

"Gintlemen and electhors! I congratulate yez most heartily upon the choice yez have made this day! yez can rest asshured that as long as the bulluk of the population constitutes the masses uv the people there will be no danger from the privileged few!"

A Novel Crime

"Not long ago," says the same judge, "a colored woman came into court to see what could be done about securing a pardon for her husband who was in jail.

"'What was your husband sentenced for?' I asked.

"'Ah ain't shuah, jedge, but ah thinks twuz emblazonment!' was the reply."

An Importunate Client

While Judge Hughes, the Prosecuting Attorney of Kansas City, was in his office one day, the voice of a negro was heard in the ante-room demanding in the name of his sovereign rights to be brought in to the official. No mere assistant would do. So they let him in.

"Ah am a taxpayer and Ah wants to see the haid man prosecutor. Ah want to get a man arrested. He done stole my money and Ah want you to get it for me."

"How did it happen?" asked the prosecutor.

"Well, Ah'm a contractor."

"What kind of a contractor?"

"A plasterin' contractor. Ah have had a colo'ed gentleman—he's the one that stole my money—and Ah paid him off. Then he went to a white man that I done some work for, and he collects the money that was coming to me."

"Let me get this straight," questioned the prosecutor with a smile. "You say that the colored gentleman—he's the thief—went to the white man—he's the man that owes you—and got the money that was due you?"

"Yessir. That's the way it is."

"You paid this colored gentleman all you owed him?"

"Yessir."

"And you didn't authorize him to collect any money for you?"

"Ah didn't do which?" asked the puzzled negro.

"You didn't authorize him."

"No," with a still more puzzled air and a scratch of the head. "Ah didn't do nothin' to him yet. But——" with a gleam in his eye that boded ill for the culprit, "Ah guess Ah'll do a little of that authorizin' when I catch that nigger."

"How much did he collect?"

"A dollah and seventy cents."

"My goodness, is that all? Well, you go right to the man who owes you and get your money. The fact that he paid some one else needn't bother you. He still owes you. If he paid the wrong man that is no concern of yours. Haven't you troubles enough of your own without having to go out and hunt them up?"

"An' Ah don't need to have him arrested?"

"No."

"Ah'm mighty thankful, mister." And the negro withdrew.

Very Indelicate

In 1881, in the Sagadahoc County court, held in the city of Bath, Maine, a case for assault and battery came up for trial: Mrs. O. vs. Mr. O.; Judge G. for plaintiff and Lawyer L. for defendant. Mr. O., by-the-way, kept a grocery store in a small country town, also the post-office in his dining and sitting-room.

Mrs. O. had testified that Mr. O. had pushed her with such violence that she fell from a platform to the ground, and injured her side in consequence of the fall, etc.

When Mr. O. came upon the stand, he swore that Mrs. O. first pushed him.

As Judge G. arose to begin the cross-examination of the defendant, Mr. O. braced up with an evident determination that the lawyer should not "browbeat" him.

Judge G. "Mr. O., what is your business or profession?"

Mr. O. "I am a merchant, sir, and a government officer, sir."

Judge G. "What office do you hold under the government?"

Mr. O. "I am the postmaster in my own town, sir."

Judge G. "Did I understand you to say that you pushed Mrs. O. down?"

Mr. O. "No, sir. I said that I pushed her, and she *fell down*. But she first pushed me."

Judge G. "How hard did she push you?"

Mr. O. "She pushed me as hard as I pushed her, sir."

Judge G. "Did you lose your equilibrium when she pushed you?"

Mr. O. "No, sir, I did *not* lose my equilibrium; I had no equilibrium to lose, for I never had any, sir (very emphatic), *and I don't think that you as a lawyer have any right to ask me any such question, sir. I consider it very indelicate.*"

Judge G. simply replied: "Oh, I beg pardon! I was not aware that you hadn't any equilibrium."

Mitigating Circumstances

The Southern darky does not always comprehend the meaning of words, and he does not always appreciate executive clemency, as witness the following incident:

"Do you plead guilty or not guilty?" asked Justice Gregg of a colored culprit, who was accused of stealing a whole line of dry goods that had been hung out in an Austin back yard to dry.

"Dat ar depends on de mitigatin' sarcumstances," responded the prisoner.

"What mitigating circumstances?"

"Well, jedge, las' time I was up heah for stealin', you said dat owin' to de mitigatin' sarcumstances ob hit bein' my fust offense, you would let me off wid a repriman'."

"Yes, and here you are again."

"Jes so, jedge. Now I wants ter know before I pleads guilty to dis heah second offense, ef you is gwine ter let me off again wid nuffin but a repriman', den I pleads guilty ter habin' lifted de line ob clothes, and while I's about it, I mout jes as well plead guilty to anudder fust offense. I refers to dat poultry Colonel Parsons missed las' week."

"Have you been guilty of any more offenses?" asked the amused justice.

"Ef I am gwine ter be let off wid a repriman', I mout as well own up ter anudder fust offense."

"What is it?"

"Four shirts, six pilly-slips, and par ob linen pants from the yard ob Mrs. Flapjack's boardin' house, and de wood pile ob Colonel Terrell in de Fust Ward."

"When were you guilty of that first offense?"

"I hain't been guilty ob dat ar fust offense at all yit. Dat ar am de fust offense I'm gwine ter to be guilty ob ter-night, or as soon as you turns me loose on account ob de mitigatin' sarcumstances."

The Judge's Queer Case

"Mister Jedge," said the old colored citizen, who came into the justice court leading a small negro boy by the coat collar, "Mister Jedge, I wish you'd please, suh, give dis boy ten years whar de State'll furnish de vittles fer him."

"What do you mean?" asked the astonished justice. "What has he been doing?"

"Eatin' me out er house en home, suh," was the reply, "wid dat ongodly appetite er his.

Why, jedge, de appetite er de whale dat swallowed Jonah couldn't hol' a candle ter dat boy's eatin' arrangements. Fer de Lawd's sake, jedge, let de State feed him a while, so's de yuther chillun kin pick up en enjoy life."

A Careful Justice

The country lawyer is apt, in the course of his general practice, to see more of the humorous side of judicial ignorance than is to be found in the somewhat more limited range of his urban brother. As an instance of this state of affairs, we give the following anecdote:

A certain suspect, in a criminal trial before a justice whose acquaintance with Blackstone would seem to be limited, having clearly established his innocence of the charge against him by an alibi, the prosecuting attorney remarked to the court:

"I think, your honor, that this trial had better stop right here. The alibi has been fully established."

"I think so myself," replied his honor, with an approving nod; and then summoning the prosecuting attorney to his side, he said, in a stage-whisper which was only too audible throughout the court-room, "I say, what is the penalty for an alibi?"

A Cool Request

At a term of the Supreme Court held in Alfred, Maine, an old gentleman who was somewhat deaf was on the witness stand. The judge had occasion to question him.

"Hey?" said the old man, his hand at the back of his ear.

The judge repeated his words, when the old gentleman innocently said, "I guess you'll have to step this way, jedge; I'm a leetle hard o' hearin'."

Senator Carmack's Little Joke

"Senator E. W. Carmack of Tennessee is quite a wag," said a former Tennessee politician recently. "About twenty years ago he was a member of the county court, of Maury County, Tennessee, and extracted a good deal of fun from the deliberations of that staid if sometimes stupid body. One of Carmack's tricks brought the court notoriety if not fame. The justices, who knew as little about the Constitution as a jaybird knows about the Koran, and cared less, were grinding out laws regulating everything under the sun. Justice Carmack arose and presented a resolution which recited in its preamble the uselessness of constitutions in general, and the depravity of the Tennessee organic law in particular, and wound up the resolve that 'the Constitution be and the same is hereby abolished.' Carmack made a brilliant and stirring speech, working the court up to a frenzy of indignation. At the close of his effort the court passed the resolution in a whoop. Nobody smiled, not even Carmack, at the time; but next day when the news was scattered broadcast, the state roared in appreciation."

Early Justice In California

A Pike County Missourian is credited with having first used the expression: "If this court knows herself, and she think she do."

Long before the discovery of gold in California, a Pike County boy named Blackburn, so it is said, ran away from home and went to the Rocky Mountains, where he grew to manhood as Indian fighter, hunter, trapper and mountain guide. He became six feet four inches tall, proportionately thin, and marvelously awkward. He had many encounters with grizzlies and Indians. He was scarred from head to foot, one eye had been partly gouged out, his hair was thin and coarse, and stood straight up on top of his head and hung in every direction from the sides. Blackburn, as might be supposed, was not an educated man, but he was not lacking in keen wit and sound sense.

When gold was discovered Blackburn went to the mines, and the miners, as a sort of joke, elected him alcalde, an office similar to that of justice of the peace. The first case brought before the alcalde was that of a gambler who, while drunk and on horseback, had run over a young Mexican woman, knocking her down and seriously injuring her. The trial took place in the largest cabin in the neighborhood, which was packed with roughly dressed, much bewhiskered men. The gambler, who was rich, hired able counsel to defend him. Alcalde Blackburn called the young woman, who told her story in broken English, but frankly and honestly. When she finished, the alcalde peremptorily ended the trial. The attorney for the defendant protested vehemently, but the alcalde ran his hand through his hair until it stood up straighter on top than ever and remarked:

"If this court knows herself, and she think she do, I fine you $500 damages and assess upon you the costs of puttin' this yer gal in good condition."

When asked what he meant by "good condition," he replied that the "gamblin' chap" must pay the doctor's bill and all other costs of the woman's illness. A more learned judge might have made a more formal ruling, but scarcely a juster one.

Legal Sore

Just after the war an old darky came up to the governor and said,—

"Marster, kin you make me jestice ob de peace?"

"Well, Uncle Ned, in a case of suicide what would you do?"

Uncle Ned thought deeply. "Marster, I'd make him pay de costs ob de court and support de child."

Had 'Em Foul

A good story of a sharp justice of the peace was told at the Galt House in St. Louis.

"It chanced," said Mr. Powhatan, "that this justice of the peace lived in a little town in a far recess of Tennessee. He was the only Republican in the district, yet he happened, by some trick of fortune, to hold office.

"At length, when political excitement had reached an unwonted pitch, a project was formed to oust him from his office and put in a Democrat.

"The election was held in an old distillery,

and the ballot box was a large gourd. The 'squire was early on the scene, clad in the roughest of clothes.

"'Fellow citizens,' he said, 'I want to make you a short speech.'

"The audience having agreed, he accordingly mounted a barrel—magnanimously determined to 'rise above all party issues and appeal to State pride and patriotism.'

"'Fellow citizens,' he said, 'I've been a-lookin' round here to see plain enough what's a-goin' on. I know what you want. I've been justice of the peace here goin' on twenty years, an' a good many times I've saved many of you from goin' to the penitentiary, an' now you're tryin' to put me out of office.

"'But I just want to tell you something. I've got the constitution and the laws of the State of Tennessee in my pocket, and just as sure as you turn me out of office I'll burn 'em up—blame me if I don't—and you may all go to ruin together.'

"The effect of the speech was overwhelming. The ruin threatener was elected by a handsome majority. To be in a state without a constitution and laws was too great a calamity to be thought of."

Could Not Appear

When Senator Burrows was practicing law in Michigan, he went one day to a court in a small town. A country lawyer was arguing before an aged and solemn justice of the peace.

"Now," said the lawyer, "if it pleases your honor, the defendant says he paid the money to the diseased, but I am goin' to show that the diseased never got the money. He didn't receive one cent, the diseased didn't ——"

"Say," broke in the justice, "what is this man diseased of? Why don't you bring him here?"

"Because, your honor, he is diseased of death."

CHAPTER XIII

Diplomacy

The Higher Strategy

SENATOR SPOONER tells of a lawyer in Wisconsin who had been retained by a farmer to prosecute a suit against a neighbor relative to the title to a strip of land running between their respective farms.

It appears that during a conversation as to the status of the suit the first-mentioned farmer suggested to his attorney that it might be a good idea to send the presiding judge a couple of fine turkeys.

"Dear me!" exclaimed the counsel, "that would never do, my man! You would be sure to lose your suit!"

Nothing more was said on the subject. The case came up, was tried, and judgment was rendered in the plaintiff's favor. When the news was brought to him the farmer expressed his satisfaction, adding: "I sent him the turkeys!"

Too astonished at the man's temerity to say

anything, the lawyer merely stared at his client.

"Yes," chuckled the farmer, "I sent him the turkeys, but I sent them in my opponent's name!"

Reduced

A few years ago the assessors of Poughkeepsie assessed some of Judge Barnard's property much higher than it had previously been assessed. He appeared in person before the assessors and endeavored to have it put back at the former valuation. He solemnly asserted to the assessors that he would accept the old assessed valuation for his property.

The assessors held their ground. One of them called on the judge later with a certified check for the amount of the assessed valuation and asked for a deed. He got it, and made $10,000 or thereabouts on the transaction at once. The judge's bluff was called—and honored.

Modest Professional Announcement

The following is on the letter-head of a "live" Western lawyer:

Am the red-headed, smooth-faced, freckle-marked legal Napoleon of the Slope, and always in the stirrups. Practice in every court on earth except that of Judge Lynch. Quick as a hippopotamus and gentle as a sunstroke. Refer to my friends and likewise to my enemies. *Fees are the sinews of war.*

The "Stovepipe Verdict"

It was a characteristic of a certain Tennessee colonel that when once his oratory had begun to flow before the jury nothing could stop it till the fount was exhausted. On one occasion he had just finished tearing his opponent's argument to tatters when the court-room stovepipe fell with a crash.

"There," cried the colonel as the clouds of soot arose, "there is a simile furnished by nature herself! Just as that stovepipe has come unjointed and fallen useless to the ground, so my adversary's argument has fallen with as loud a crash. One is not more hollow than the other, nor more in need of polish.

"And, gentlemen of the jury, what do those clouds of soot and smoke resemble,—those black masses smutting all they light upon,—what do they resemble more than the malicious libels, the black scandals which my adversary has poured into your ears, and with which he has endeavored to blacken the character of my client?"

His case had seemed hopeless, but when he

had finished the stovepipe comparison the jury was converted, and returned what became famous in western Tennessee as the "stovepipe verdict" in favor of the colonel's client.

Old-Time Lawyers

"The old-time vitriolic lawyer, the picturesque character who stormed up and down the circuits, roaring at courts, juries and especially at witnesses, seems in these degenerate times to have given place to a successor who is almost effeminate in comparison," said one of the veterans of the Kansas bar. "When I entered on practice thirty-one years ago, the late Judge John W. Henry, of Kansas City, was on the bench of the Twenty-seventh, as this judicial circuit was then numbered. Around him was an array of Blackstonian disciples brave as lions and apparently as fierce in action. Out of court they were the most jolly, companionable men that ever clinked glasses across the board. Their examination of witnesses was a fight from start to finish. They prided themselves upon being 'severe.' They were quick and abrupt. They terrified the most self-possessed of witnesses. With finger poised like a rifle, face intense and rebuking, a lawyer would put the questions like a monk of the inquisition.

"I cannot account for the practice unless it was to impress the spectators and reporters. As a rule, harsh conduct by a lawyer wins sympathy from the jury adverse to his cause. You will notice by an examination of verdicts that the case winners before juries are men of urbanity. I know an instance where a case was won by a lawyer's refusal to condemn a witness who had evidently perjured himself.

"'Why in the mischief didn't you roast that fellow as he deserved?' demanded his associate counsel. 'You handled him as if you were afraid of him.'

"'Didn't the examination convince you he was lying?' the mild lawyer asked.

"'Yes, but why didn't you rub it in while you had him at your mercy?'

"'Because the jurymen are the ones to fix the penalty. All I had to do was to establish his guilt.'"

The Way to Swear

There was once in a certain Minnesota county, as clerk of the District Court, an intelligent and careful German, who during the sessions of the court was very fastidious about violations of decorum. Recently in an important trial a somewhat "bumptious" young man from the rural districts was called as a witness, and took his place on the stand without removing his hat. He was told to hold up his hand, which he did, and the clerk proceeded to administer the customary oath, reading it from the statute. He had read about half way through, when, happening to glance up over his spectacles, he noticed that the witness had not removed his hat. The clerk slowly lowered the book, and gazing intently at the young man, said, "*Look here, sir, when you swear before me and Gott, take off your hat, sir!*"

A Strong Argument

In the course of the trial of a lawsuit against a horse railway in New York, the leading counsel for the losing side, a robust and witty Irishman, endeavored to work on the sympathies of the jury by calling attention to the ease with which corporations obtained franchises from an alleged corrupt Legislature.

"Whoy, gintlemin uv th' joory," he said, impressively, "in these days phin fran-*chises* are given away at Albany, ony man can get a fran-*chise* to run a harse railway onypheres. Indade, gintlemin, it would not surphrise me to hear at ony toime that me learned fri'nd, the coun-*sel* for the opposition, had got a fran-*chise* to run a harse railway down me spoine, wid th' privilege uv usin' me ribs for switchus."

Mr. March's Chinook Testimony

In a dispute between the Indians and the cannery men in Seattle, Wash., a Mr. March was called as a witness, and the way in which he gave testimony proved puzzling to the lawyers.

"How long have you been in this part of the country, Mr. March?"

"Forty, forty-five, fifty, fifty-five years."

"Fifty-five years," said the lawyer, and then, as if he were addressing Christopher Columbus, he asked:

"And what did you discover, Mr. March?"

"A dark-visaged savage."

"Dark-visaged savage, eh? Yes, and what did you say to him?"

"I said it was a fine day."

"Fine day? Yes, and what did he say to you?"

Mr. March rattled off a whole yarn in Chinook, and kept on, to the mirth of the whole court-room, until peremptorily cut off by the gavel of the judge.

"I asked you what reply the savage made to you, Mr. March. Please answer the question," said the irate cross-examiner.

"I was answering."

"Tell us what the savage said?"

"That was what he said."

"Then tell it to us in English."

"Not unless I am commissioned by the court to act as an interpreter and paid the customary fee."

The lawyer thought a moment, looked at the judge, who could not resist a smile, and said severely: "Mr. March, you may stand down."

Got His Client Off

They tell a good story at the expense of W. B——, the only lawyer at the A—— County bar, or in the United States, for that matter, who holds the distinction of having been city attorney of the three most important cities of one county at various times. He was counsel some time ago for a man charged with a serious offense, and on the day of the trial the defendant was in a condition that would certainly not have improved his chances of acquittal. Attorney B—— was worried, but he is a general in addition to being a political diplomat. He locked his client into a room in a down-town hotel and then studied out the knotty problem before him.

One of the most prominent oil operators of

Pittsburg, and one of his most intimate friends, happened into his office shortly before he was ready to try the case. It was only a social call for a quiet chat, and Mr. B—— requested that his friend go into the court-room with him. The oil operator sat beside Mr. B—— at the counsel table, and, during the progress of the case, he took little note of what was going on. He was not interested. Several times witnesses pointed in his direction, as did Mr. B——, but the oil operator thought nothing of it. Mr. B—— tried to be indifferent. None of the witnesses appeared to know the operator, at least they said that they did not, and the prosecutor also stated that he did not know the man seated beside Mr. B——. The jury naturally thought the man was Mr. B——'s client, and when the district attorney, at the conclusion of the testimony, got up and said, "That is my case; this is not the man," not many minutes were wasted in bringing in a verdict of acquittal.

The oil operator accompanied Mr. B—— out of court, and it was not until they were a safe distance away from the seat of justice that Mr. B—— confided to his friend that he had posed as the defendant in the case. The operator was mad all through when he first heard of it, but the ridiculousness of the situation appealed to him and he took it as a huge joke and as a sample of the diplomacy of one who could pull a brand out of the burning. It is doubtful whether the brilliant city attorney would acknowledge the story, but his friends say it is true.

Successful Gallantry

A justice of the peace had just finished the ceremony and was looking at the happy couple in a smilingly expectant manner.

"Are we married?" the bridegroom inquired.

"You are," the justice replied.

"Firm and tight?"

"As tight as the law can bind you."

"Then," said the bridegroom, "I'm sorry to say that I haven't a cent to pay you. I'll have to see you later."

The justice frowned. He had counted on two dollars at least.

"I don't know about that," he said. "My terms are cash, and if you can't pay I'll have to find some means of declaring this contract not binding and of no effect. Let me see. I have it. You have grossly misrepresented the lady's age. You told me she was twenty-six, when anybody can see that she isn't a day over seventeen."

Whereupon the bride, who was nearly forty, felt so much gratitude that she promptly paid the justice out of her own pocket.

Saw Wood and Say Nothing

A lawyer still living at White Plains once called at Judge Barnard's house at Poughkeepsie to procure the judge's signature to an exparte order. He found the judge in his back yard, sawing wood, and after explaining the nature of his errand offered the remark that the judge was indulging in good healthy exercise.

"Do you think so?" responded the judge in an instant. "Well, you use the saw while I go in and look over your papers."

The White Plains lawyer vows that the judge took precisely the time to look over his papers that it took him to finish all the wood in the pile to be sawed. And he had a vague impression that the judge was watching him through the shutters all the time.

A Police Court Scene

The police court has always had a peculiar fascination for loafers. At nine o'clock in the morning you can see the corridor shark, the police court attorney, and the unfortunate client, all engaged in earnest conversation. The police court shyster is invariably a shabby genteel individual who knows everything but law, but he is possessed of a very loud voice, which by the illiterate and ill-informed is always considered the standard of a first-class lawyer.

The judge has ascended the bench, and the hearing of applications for warrants is in progress. His honor, with a good-natured Hibernian accent, remarks: "What is the trouble today, Officer McGrath?" "Your honor, I've arrested a man for having four wives." "Ah, let me see what we shall charge him with," remarks his honor.

"Hould, I have it. The first marriage is called in law 'matrimony,' the second 'bigamy,' the third 'polygamy,' and the fourth 'ignominy.' Poor fellow, I may sind to the grand jury a recommendation for mercy. It wasn't his fault that there were any old maids in the country."

"Officer Duffy, what can the court do for you this mornin'?" "Your honor, some boys set off firecrackers which were tied to the tail of Paddy O'Rourke's coat." "Let me see. This question is a perplexing one. Ah, I have it! Let me look into a book which I am told contains the law on all subjects. It is called 'Every Man His Own Lawyer, or the Practice of Law

Made Aisy.' It contains 200,000 statements of the law, and 430,000 offenses against the law and their remedies. Let me look under Tinaments and Hereditaments. These boys must be complained of for malicious injury to Paddy O'Rourke's tinaments. A tinament is something that adjoins, and as his coat was adjoining his person, it is clearly a tinament according to my judgment."

"Officer Gillespie, what can the court do for you this mornin'?" "This woman, your honor, wants her husband arrested for non-support." "Well, madam, what did your husband do?" "He forgot to give me his pay envelope Saturday night." "But this is only Monday," remarked his honor. "It's the beginning of a bad habit," replied the woman. "Well," replied his honor in a sympathetic tone, "perhaps your husband had a bad memory; it may be pure forgetfulness on his part." "Bad luck to him, your honor, he remembers the day he first met me, the day he proposed, the day of our wedding, my birthday, and the age of the baby when he cut his first tooth. Do you call that a bad mimory?" His honor acknowledged defeat and granted the warrant.

CHAPTER XIV

In Rural Districts

He Stopped Interruptions

"THE practice of law in the country may not be so lucrative as in the big city, but it is vastly more amusing," said a lawyer of prominence in Oswego. "One experience rewarded me for all the trouble I had in getting to the scene of the trial.

"The case was going along smoothly and I was examining an important witness, when from the rear of the crowded court room this remark was interjected in a loud voice:

"'That man's a liar.'

"I hesitated a moment, expecting the judge, a bluff country jurist, to take some action. He said nothing, so I continued to question the man on the stand.

"Presently came another outburst from the voice in the crowd. It was to the effect that the witness had no truth in his make-up and his story was an offense against justice. Still the judge said not a word.

"Feeling that it was up to me to do something, I asked the judge to have the person who dared to interrupt the proceedings committed for contempt. The judge leaned over to me and whispered:

"'I'd do it, counselor, but I don't know how to draw the papers.'

"The judge may have been weak on law, but he was strong on human nature. He pondered a moment and then turned to the witness, who was a big chap.

"'Do you know who it was that called you a liar?' he asked.

"'I do, your honor,' said the witness.

"'Can you lick him?' the judge queried.

"'That's what I can.'

"'Then you go and do it,' ordered his honor. 'This court is adjourned for fifteen minutes until this little matter is adjusted.'

"The witness left the chair, singled out a pugnacious looking but under-sized man in the crowd, grabbed him by the collar and yanked him out into the sunlight. In five minutes the witness was back, slightly ruffled in his appearance, but smiling broadly. He resumed his place on the stand, the judge rapped for order, and the trial of the case went on.

"There were no more interruptions."

Gave the Court Notice

In a rural justice court the defendant in a case was sentenced to serve thirty days in jail. He had known the judge from boyhood, and addressed him as follows:

"Bill, old boy, you're a gwine ter send me ter jail, air you?"

"That's what," replied the judge. "Have you got anything to say agin it?"

"Only this here, Bill: God help you when I git out!"

A Virginia Daniel Come to Judgment

Judge Crutchfield was credited with a sharper wit than any jurist in Virginia. On one occasion he had two cases before him, one being that of "Red" Foster of the Richmond baseball team and the other that of a man charged with picking pockets. The judge was a baseball enthusiast, and Foster's case was called first, in order that the baseball player might get into a game which the judge intended to see. The testimony was conclusive, and "Red" was fined ten dollars for striking a negro.

"If you could hit the ball, 'Red,' as hard as you hit that black man you'd be a star," remarked his honor.

The pickpocket then came up and pleaded

not guilty; but he was friendless and the judge said that he was a suspicious character anyway, and fined him ten dollars. The unfortunate fellow said that he had only seven dollars in his possession, whereupon the judge said to the bailiff:

"Turn this man loose in this crowd, and if he doesn't raise enough in half an hour to pay his fine he is innocent; let him go."

By picking no pockets for half an hour the fellow proved his innocence and was discharged.

Established His Identity

In a court room of one of the Blue Grass counties of Kentucky, General H——, a prominent lawyer of that region, was defending a prisoner charged with horse stealing, and the witness was swearing as to the identity of the stolen horse.

"How do you know this is the same horse?" asked General H——.

"Why, I just know it is," said the witness.

"Well how?" again asked General H——.

"I can't tell exactly how; but I know it as well as I know you, General H——."

"Well, how do you know that I am General H——?"

"Because just before dinner I heard Mr.

C—— say, 'General H——, let's go and take a drink,' and you went."

Knowing Old Man

An old miner once visited a lawyer to make his will. The old man's property consisted of two small cottages which had cost him $400. The lawyer asked him how he wished to dispose of it.

"Ma auld woman is to hev it all so long as she's ma widow; after that, bairns to hev all," said the client.

"What age is your wife?" asked the lawyer.

"Seventy-two," was the reply.

'And how long have you been married?" was the next question.

"Over fifty years," was the reply.

The lawyer suggested that under the circumstances he should let his wife have the little property during her life, whether she remained a widow or not.

"Aa winnot! Aa winnot!" exclaimed the old man. "Aa'll hev me aan way!"

"But surely," expostulated the lawyer, "you don't expect an old woman now over seventy-two would ever dream of marrying again?"

The miner looked the lawyer full in the face and answered very solemnly:

"Well, sonny, there's na knowing what young chaps like yoursel' will dae for money!"

Confirmed the Judge's View

Judge Kennedy of the Newton police court, although a model of courtesy on the bench, never fails to nail a lie, especially if the falsifier is on trial for a crime.

An old offender was arraigned before him, charged with drunkenness. When the complaint had been read the defendant bravely answered, "Not guilty." The judge, eying him sharply, inquired: "How long since you were drunk?" The prisoner answered that he had not taken a drink for more than a year.

"That's not true," replied his honor. "I saw you drunk within a month on the street in Boston, and you had the impudence to accost me."

"Did I spake to you, sor?" asked the prisoner.

"You did," said the judge.

"Well, thin, I must have been drunk, yer anner."

No one in the court room enjoyed the incident more than the judge.

An Expert Decision

Champ Clark tells of a suit in which he was retained that was tried in a "country justice shop" in Missouri.

"The opposing party," says Mr. Clark, "had sued my client outside of the township in which he lived, so I 'took the statute' with me to have the case dismissed for want of jurisdiction. The local justice of the peace was a shoemaker. His office was in his shoe shop, and the son of Crispin sat on his bench among his leathers and his tools attentively listening to my reading of the law and the motion to dismiss the case. Upon the termination of my little argument the justice shoemaker showed signs of indecision. With an owlish air of wisdom he informed me that he had his doubts as to that statute; furthermore, he intimated that it would be well to go slow where 'these city lawyers' were concerned. Finally he threw aside a boot he had been pegging and announced:

"'Well, sir, I've got to see Squire Johnson about this. You take the bench, Squire Morton, till I get back.'

"So off he went to get the opinion of a veteran local lawyer, the legal authority of the town. Mr. Morton, the other legal magnate he had addressed, gravely took the bench and held it till the justice returned. In fact, he held it longer, for it proved a matter of considerable difficulty to separate him from it. When he tried to rise there was an awful clatter of knives, brad-awls, shoes and leather—the bench rose with him. It appeared that the worthy man had become attached to it by contact with a piece of cobbler's wax on which he had inadvertently sat. After a while the separation was effected, when the justice resumed his seat and solemnly announced:

"'The case is dismissed.'"

Strong Suspicion

Not long ago a man was charged at a country court with trespassing, and also with shooting a number of pigeons, the property of a local farmer.

In giving his evidence the farmer was exceedingly careful, even nervous, and the lawyer for the defense endeavored to frighten him.

"Now," he remarked, sternly, "remember you're on oath! Are you prepared to swear that this man shot your pigeons?"

"I didn't say he did shoot 'em," was the reply. "I said I suspected him of doing it."

"Ah! Now we're coming to it. What made you suspect the man?"

"Well, firstly, I caught him on my land with a gun. Secondly, I'd heard a gun go off and had seen some pigeons fall. Thirdly, I found four of my pigeons in his pocket—and I don't think them birds flew into his pocket and committed suicide for the fun of the thing."

The Truth Came Out

The following comes from a well-known lawyer in one of the rural districts of Pennsylvania:

A young man was charged with forging the will of a lady, which devised to him a considerable amount of her property; but, as the case proceeded, it became clear to me that the will was signed after the lady's death, and then with a dry pen held in the hand of the deceased by the accused himself while he guided it over a signature which he had craftily forged. A woman was present when this was done, and as she had attested the execution of the will, she was a necessary witness for the prisoner, and in examination-in-chief she was very clear indeed that it was by the hand of the deceased that the will was signed, and that she herself had seen the deceased sign it. Suspicion only existed as to what the real facts were until this woman went into the box, and then a scene, highly dramatic, occurred in her cross-examination.

After getting an admission that the will was signed in the bed, with the prisoner near by, the woman was asked :

"Did he put the pen into her hand?"

"Yes."

"And assist her while she signed the will?"

"Yes."

"How did he assist her?"

"By raising her in the bed and supporting her when he had raised her."

"Did he guide her hand?"

"No."

"Did he touch her hand at all?"

"I think he did just touch her hand."

"When he did touch her hand, was she dead?"

At this last question the woman turned terribly pale, was seen to falter, and fell in a swoon on the ground and so revealed the truth which she had come to deny.

'Way Down East

An Englishman while passing along the main street in a small town in Maine stepped in a hole in the sidewalk and, falling, broke his leg. He brought suit against the city for one thousand dollars, and engaged Hannibal Hamlin for counsel. Hamlin won his case, but the city appealed to the supreme court. Here also the decision was for Hamlin's client.

After settling up the claim, Hamlin sent for his client and handed him one dollar.

"What's this?" asked the Englishman.

"That's your damages, after taking out my fee, the cost of appeal, and several other expenses," said Hamlin.

The Englishman looked at the dollar and then at Hamlin. "What's the matter with this?" he asked; "is it bad?"

Blasphemous Defense

An amusing instance of how ignorant some country magistrates can be when legal knowledge is required has recently leaked out in a borough not forty miles from New York.

A gentleman of a legal frame of mind, taking a short trip by boat, failed to show his ticket, which the wind had suddenly blown out of his hand. It was never denied that he had purchased one for the journey, but, being unable to produce the ticket, and unwilling to buy another, he was accordingly summoned to the local court.

The defendant pleaded the adequate, even if ingenious, defense that it was "an act of God." The judge inflicted a rather heavy fine, and it is positively stated that he considered the defense gross blasphemy.

The Foreman's Smile

"Some time ago," says Mr. J. O. Lydick, "I was called in to attend a boy charged, in the mayor's court in the town of Wayne, Indian Territory, with the crime of petit larceny, the theft of some cheap jewelry. The town had just been incorporated, although it had stood there for twenty years, and this was the first case to be tried in the new court. Men had grown from childhood to gray haired grandfathers in that community and had never seen a court or attended an election. This was a great occasion to them. In order that weighty business affairs might not detain them the hearing of this case was arranged for the evening. The supper hour was scarcely passed when great throngs of people came, all anxious to hear a case in court and talking of the importance of elections. I heard some talk of the evidence, the fate of my client, but continually would I hear comment upon the election and the chances of different persons whose names were new and strange to me. I couldn't understand this election talk, and didn't understand it until the whole thing was over and success attained.

"A jury had been selected and was at once impaneled. The evidence was introduced and we argued the case. Opposing counsel and myself were watched and our attempts at wit applauded. The case concluded, the jury, duly impressed with the great responsibility resting upon them, retired to deliberate. It was two o'clock A. M. and it was very dark. Time passed, three o'clock came, then 3:30, and no verdict. The anxiety and excitement grew intense, and faces grew pale and haggard. The mother of the poor boy whose fate rested with the absent jury, and who, if convicted, might possibly have to pay a fine of ten dollars, swooned, and fell to the floor. The most careful attention of the city doctor barely restored her, and, as time passed and yet no verdict, the anxiety almost changed to remorse. The scene was like that of a death chamber, and the sacredness of the occasion was only interrupted by men on the outside betting on that election which I heard so much of but could not understand.

"Then just as the first rays of day came gleaming faintly through the windows the door opened and the jury entered. All was breathless silence now. The jury looked tired and all were gloomy save the one juror who proudly walked at the head of that august procession of twelve. This gentleman, with a smile upon his face like that of one who had achieved greatness, handed the verdict to the court, and his honor the mayor, to the anxious and eager-faced audience, read:

"'We, the jury, duly impaneled to try the above entitled case, find the defendant not guilty. Eli Crookedwolf, foreman.'

"The boy yelled and jumped over the stove; the fainting mother screamed and cried with joy; men in wild voices called for the stake money; and a hundred men wild with excitement ran over me before I could get out of the way. Then some came to congratulate me upon my victory, but I saw the whole crowd gathered around that smiling juror, yelling three cheers for Mr. Eli Crookedwolf, the foreman; he was the recipient of the greatest honors of the occasion. I didn't understand until I approached the dejected eleven remaining jurors and, through idle curiosity, inquired, 'What made you so long reaching a verdict?' when they all simultaneously responded:

"'Verdict, eh? We never did have any trouble about a verdict. We all agreed on the first ballot that he was not guilty, but we did have the goldarndest time you ever saw electing a foreman, and it took three hours and forty-seven ballots for Eli Crookedwolf to win out.'

"And then I understood that election talk and why Mr. Crookedwolf wore the smile."

He Told Him How Old the Barn Was

The old practice of badgering witnesses has almost disappeared, but in some country districts it is still kept up—sometimes, however, to the damage of the cross-examiner.

Lawyer S—— is well-known for his uncomely habits. He cuts his hair about four times a year, and the rest of the time looks decidedly ragged about the ears. He was making a witness describe a barn which figured in his last case.

"How long had the barn been built?"

"Oh, I don't know. About a year, mebby. About nine months, p'r'aps."

"But just how long? Tell the jury how long it had been built."

"Well, I don't know exactly. Quite a while."

"Now, Mr. B——, you pass for an intelligent farmer, and yet you can't tell me how old this barn is; and you have lived on the next farm for ten years. Can you tell me how old your own barn is? Come, now, tell me how old your own barn is, if you think you know."

Quick as lightning the old farmer replied:

"Ye want to know how old my barn is, do ye? Well, it's just about as old as you be, and needs the roof seeing to about as bad."

In the roar that followed the witness stepped down, and Lawyer S—— did not call him back.

Why He Passed

One of Assistant Attorney-General Beck's stories was especially appreciated by law students. A general in the Civil War applied at the close of the conflict for admission to the bar of the United States.

A committee of three examiners reported that he had answered correctly two-thirds of the questions put to him. A judge, astonished at the general's success, asked the chairman of the committee what the questions were.

"Well," he replied, "the first was, 'What is the rule in Shelly's case?' and the answer was 'Writing poetry.' That was not correct.

"Then we asked him what was a 'contingent remainder' and a 'vested interest,' and he said he did not know. That was correct, and we admitted him."

They Discovered a Loophole

Not far below Augusta, Georgia, the Savannah River is crossed by an antiquated flatboat, hanging by a cable from a post far up-stream, and impelled from bank to bank by the action of the current. This is the "Sand-bar Ferry," and from time immemorial until the abolition of dueling, the banks of the river on both sides were bloody fields of so-called honor.

Gentlemen of South Carolina, having quarreled, crossed in the rickety flatboat with their seconds and fought their battles on Georgia soil, and Georgians went over to the Palmetto State for their shooting or sword-play.

Thither, one day, went a solemn procession of principals, seconds and witnesses, most of them representatives of the Georgia bar. They were more solemn than usual, for the fight they were to witness was to wipe out the most terrible of insults. Two well-known lawyers of Rome, who had been lifelong friends, had fallen out, and one of them, in the height of a dispute, had reviled the other with all the terrible words he could lay tongue to.

There had been a score of men present to hear and to prevent an immediate shooting, and now the two devoted friends, turned enemies, rode with their party toward the fatal ground where they were to make target-practice on each other. Each of them was downcast and gloomy, for at heart they were devoted. But the insult was deadly, and there seemed no escape with honor from the encounter.

When they arrived at the ferry, however, the flatboat was on the other side. A second picked up the horn from the post and blew it lustily. Over and over he sounded it, until from a distant field the aged ferryman came sauntering leisurely down to his craft. The two lawyers sat side by side on their horses and watched his slow progress. The strain grew momentarily heavier and the men gloomier. At last one of them—the insulted—could stand it no longer.

"Jim," he said, impulsively, "before we go out of Georgia I want you to answer me one question. How did you ever come to apply all those epithets to me?"

"Charley," said Jim, solemnly, "I did it in my professional capacity."

The face of the man who had been insulted lighted up with a smile of great relief, and he held out his hand.

"I knew it! I knew it!" he cried. "Shake on it! Who ever heard of holding a lawyer responsible for what he said in his professional capacity? It would be madness, sir, madness!"

They shook hands fervently and the duel was declared off.

How Old-Time Lawyer Got an Acquittal

"Old-time lawyers in our state still recount with glee how a shrewd member of the bar saved a client from the penitentiary," said M. W. Hastings, of Alabama.

"This lawyer had been employed by a tough citizen to defend him on a charge of horse stealing. The State had a strong case, and it looked as though with such positive proof the accused was certain to go behind the bars. Now at that period the law was such that a man could only be tried on an original indictment; in other words, if an indictment were lost or destroyed the result was the same as an acquittal. Desperate conditions require desperate remedies, and what does this lawyer for the defense do, after making a pretext of wishing to examine the document, but sit there in the court room and deliberately chew up that indictment and swallow the fragments.

"And this was the cause of a change in the statutes of Alabama, whereby a new or substitute indictment can be got out and held as valid in case of the disappearance of the original."

Courtship Decision in Pennsylvania

A Montgomery County judge has rendered an important decision—of especial interest to girls. He has declared that it was not an offense for a girl to sit on her lover's lap, and in charging the jury said: "If every girl in Montgomery County who sits upon her lover's lap were to be judged of ill repute, we should have to blush for our county." That judge is all right.

Getting Older

James Whitcomb Riley says that he was summoned as a witness in a case tried in an Indiana rural court where one of the witnesses before him evinced some disinclination to state her age.

"Is it very necessary?" coyly asked the witness, a spinster of uncertain age.

"It is absolutely necessary, madam," interposed the judge.

"Well," sighed the maiden, "if I must I suppose I must. I didn't see how it could possibly affect the case, for you see ——"

"Madam," observed the judge, with some asperity, "I must ask you not to further waste the time of this court. Kindly state your age."

Whereupon the spinster showed signs of hysterics. "I am, that is, I was ——"

"Madam, hurry up!" exclaimed the judge, now thoroughly impatient. "Every minute makes it worse, you know!"

Little in Much

In a small country town the clerk to the magistrate is much addicted to legal phraseology, and the rustics brought before the bench are often quite aghast when they hear their offenses set forth in legal diction.

Not long ago a man had struck his neighbor, who had summoned him for the offense, and when the case came before the magistrate the clerk read the indictment as follows:

"That you, Edward Jones, willfully and with malice aforethought and prepense, did assail, attack, assault, beat, batter, or otherwise maltreat one William B——, with intent to do the said William B—— bodily harm, mischief, or injury, contrary to the statute in such case made and provided."

"Are you guilty or not guilty?" asked the clerk.

"What! Doin' all that?" exclaimed the astonished offender.

"Yes; guilty or not guilty?"

"Why, I only punched Bill's head!"

The Court Milked the Cow

"The court will proceed to milk this cow and judicial notice will be taken of those facts which to him as an expert milker will tend to determine whether she has been fresh for a long or a short time."

So announced Judge John F. Oliver after hearing witnesses dispute for an hour concerning the identity of a Jersey cow. Both sides claimed her; but one side contended that she had been fresh only three months, while the other alleged that she had not been fresh for nearly a year.

The court adjourned to a stable near by, where his honor proceeded to milk the cow in true farmer fashion.

"The verdict of the court is that the cow has not been fresh over three months; therefore she goes to the plaintiff," was the announcement from the bench after the court had solemnly led the procession back to the court-house.

Willing to Pay for His Contempt

The following anecdote is told of Gen. Gilman Marston, a once famous New Hampshire lawyer:

General Marston was attending court at a small country town when a young attorney made a motion that was denied by the court. The young man remonstrated against what he thought was the wrong ruling of the judge. So vehemently did he do so that he was fined ten dollars for contempt of court. An older attorney took the matter up, and he was fined a similar sum. Still another, who thought he stood a little better with the judge, endeavored to straighten the matter out, but he too enriched the coffers of the State by paying a "ten spot" for contempt.

General Marston was then seen to rise in his seat and advance to the clerk's desk. Taking his long pocketbook from his pocket he took out two ten dollar bills and laid them on the desk.

"What is that for?" said the judge.

"I want you distinctly to understand," said the general, "that I have just twice as much contempt for this d—— court as any man here, and I am paying for it."

Killing Two Birds with One Stone

In a businesslike way a woman from the country who entered a Muskegon lawyer's office, together with a young couple, explained that the object of the visit was to have an application for a divorce drawn up.

The attorney ventured to remark that the couple looked too young to think of separation, but the older woman explained that it was she who wanted the divorce; that the young lady was her daughter, who had just secured a marriage license to wed the young man at her side. She had been wanting to get a divorce for some time, she said, but hated to spare the time to come to town. However, her daughter having decided on matrimony, and being too young to secure the license without parental consent, she had to come anyhow, and could thus give her consent to her daughter's marriage and begin a divorce for herself.

An Apt Reference

An instance of legal courtesy occurred not long ago in a Western court room. A lawyer with Mac prefaced to his name and a brother lawyer engaged in a heated discussion. The latter maintained his position, claiming he could find his authority, and began to turn over the pages of the statute book when quick as a flash Mac said: "You will find what you want on page —, section —."

Mac's opponent looked up the reference and found the law governing idiots.

CHAPTER XV

The Negro and the Law

He Pled Guilty

THE scene was in the court room in Manatee County, Florida. The sheriff had called the witnesses in the case of the State against Abe Johnson. The State had announced ready for trial and the judge had directed that the prisoner be arraigned. He was a short and very black, chunky darky, clothed in garments of broadcloth which had evidently belonged one hundred years before to some white man of twice his size and girth. He was charged with pig stealing—the greatest offense known to Florida law, for it is generally known and understood that while a jury will not find a man guilty of murder they will surely find him guilty of pig stealing. The prisoner pleaded not guilty in his own manner and words, which were: "Wha' dat yo' scuses me of? Stealin' a hawg? No, jedge, I didn't do it." The judge asked him if he had counsel, and after the judge explained to him that counsel meant a lawyer, he said: "No, sah, I ain't got none, jedge." The judge asked him if he would like to have counsel appointed, and he said: "I's got no money, jedge, to pay 'im." The judge then said that he would appoint a lawyer to defend him, if he hadn't the money, without charge, and casting his eye over the court room he called upon a young lawyer just admitted and said: "Mr. Thompson, will you defend this man?" The prisoner cast his eye upon his counsel and then upon the court, and before anything else was said the prisoner remarked: "Jedge, you 'p'int dat man to 'fend me?" "Yes." "Well, den, jedge, I pleads guilty and throws myself on de ignorance ob dis court." And the laugh that followed touched the judge's heart, and made what might have been a penitentiary term a short jail sentence.

Getting Things Right

The juryman with the whiskers again assumed a judicial air and butted in.

"And you say he hurled invectives at you?" he demanded.

The plaintiff looked reluctant.

"No, boss," he replied. "To tell the hones' truth, it was on'y clam shells he threw at me, but what I'se kickin' about is the drefful way he cussed me ever' time I dodged 'em."

Charge as He Remembered It

Judge Brady had a colored man before him in a police court and he asked him when he had been arrested before. The fellow scratched his head, thought a moment, and then said: "Ah think it was about a year ago, jedge."

"What was the charge?" asked the court.

After thinking a while the prisoner looked up and said: "Ah'm not quite shuah, but ah t'ink it was t'ree dollahs, yer honah."

He was discharged.

Not His Friend

One morning as Justice Friedel was seated at his desk at the Eastern police station, Baltimore, busily engaged in filling out the commitments, he was suddenly disturbed by an airy young negro who brushed into the room and without more ado blurted out:

"Mohnin', Squiah. I wants a warrant for a niggah who broke the peace last night by strikin' me on mah head with a brick. I didn't do nothin' to him. He jes' hit me, dat's all."

After inquiry Justice Friedel decided that he could issue the warrant, and forthwith began to fill out the warrant blank.

"What's your name?" inquired the magistrate.

"Charles Sewell, yo' honah," came the prompt response, "an' his name is Thomas Kane," Sewell continued, as Justice Friedel began to write.

"What did you say your friend's name is?" asked the justice.

"Fren'? Fren'?" grunted the complainant. "He ain' no fren' of mine. He hit me with a brick."

Divided with the Jury

Pompey to-day is a familiar figure among the colored citizens of a town in southern Georgia, though his appearances in court to answer for petty thefts are less frequent than in the days of his youth.

On one occasion Pompey was arraigned for stealing a dozen or more watermelons from a neighbor's patch.

He appeared calm and unconcerned in court while his lawyer spoke in his defense, and, later, when the jury rendered the verdict "Not guilty," Pompey's white teeth glistened as he lapsed into an expansive smile of complete satisfaction.

As he turned to leave the court room the judge, who was well acquainted with the old negro's tricks, said: "Now, Pompey, I believe that you did steal those melons, despite the jury's opinion on the subject."

Pompey scratched his woolly head meditatively, and then drawled: "Yas, sir, yas, sir, jedge, you sho' is right; hit's jes' as you say; I sutenly did jes' natchelly use persuasion wid dem millons; but you see, jedge, de jury dey help eat 'em."

A Public Servant

The feeling in the South toward the negro when he performs any of the official functions which were formerly reserved for the white man is illustrated by a story which is told by a North Carolina gentleman.

"Jim Blank," said he, "is a very decent negro in our county, and a little while ago we made him sheriff. He was as surprised as anybody when the votes were counted and he was found to have won the election. He could not have won it except for a generous white support.

"Jim had worked at one time for a former white sheriff, and had seen his methods, having helped him on one or two occasions to bring negro offenders to jail. Now, the way an officer of the law arrests a negro down in our country is to walk up to him and say, 'Bill, you nigger, put your hands together, and do it quick!' Then he slips the wristlets on.

"Well, Jim hadn't been in office a month before he was sent to arrest a white citizen. Being a pretty intelligent fellow, he was a good deal puzzled to know what he should do, as he realized that a white man would not relish being taken into custody by him. So he came to me for counsel.

"I was busy, and, without thinking much about it, dismissed him quickly, saying, 'Why, Jim, you've seen Sheriff Dash arrest men! Just go ahead and do the way he did.' Heaven forgive me for giving such advice to my poor black friend! My goodness! You ought to have seen the riot Jim raised by following my advice literally.

"Jim was awfully cut up by the result of the experiment, and steered clear of me when he set out in search of consolation. But he went to a colored neighbor and poured out his troubles.

"'Psho!' said his friend. 'Jim, you ought to know better'n to talk to a white man as if he was a niggah. What you ought to done was to go up to him and say, "Excuse me, Mistah Jones, but would you mind jest steppin' up to the co't-house a minute? The jedge p'sents his compliments, and'll be glad to see yuh if yuh ain't no mo' pressin' business on hand.''' "

A True Definition

Judge Clayton, of Alabama, tells of a case in a court of that state, in which the first witness called was an aged darky.

Before he was sworn the presiding magistrate directed that the usual question be put to the negro, "Do you know the nature of an oath?"

The old darky shifted himself from one foot to the other before replying. A sly grin crept into his face. "Well, jedge," said he, "I cain't say how 'tis wid mos' folks; but, yo' honah, I reckon it's sorter secon' nature wid me."

One on the "Jedge"

A corpulent negro woman came into the office of Judge George I. Griffith, of Kansas City, Kansas, one morning and inquired for the "jedge."

"What can I do for you?" asked the judge.

"Is yoh runnin' foh jedge agin?" she asked.

"Yes, I'm trying to get the nomination," the judge replied.

"What's the 'sideration foh votes dis yeah?"

"What!" almost yelled the judge, beginning to understand the drift of the conversation.

"Ah means," explained the negress, "is votes wuth one dollah er two dollahs dis 'lection?"

"Are you aware that it is a serious offense for a person to sell his vote?" sternly demanded the judge.

"Ah don't 'zactly undahstan' yoh langwidge, jedge, but ef yoh means yoh ain't buyin' 'em, dat's all right. Ah believe you'se no politishun nohow." And with this contemptuous parting shot she left the office.

Couldn't Corner Sam

Jim Webster was being tried for bribing a colored witness, Sam Johnsing, to testify falsely.

"You say the defendant offered you $50 to testify in his behalf?"

"Yes, sah."

"Now repeat what he said, using his exact words."

"He said he would give me $50 if I——"

"He didn't speak in the third person, did he?"

"No, sah; he tuck good care dat dar was no third person around; dar was only two—us two."

"I know that, but he spoke to you in the first person, didn't he?"

"I was the first pusson myself."

"You don't understand me. When he was talking to you did he say, 'I will pay you $50'?"

"No, sah; he didn't say nothin' 'bout you payin' me $50. Your name wasn't mentioned, 'ceptin' he told me ef eber I got into a scrape you was de best lawyer in San Antonio to fool de jedge an' de jury—in fac', you was de best in town to cover up rascality."

For a brief breathless moment the trial was suspended.

The Lawyer's Fault

Senator Blackburn says that once when a joint committee of the Louisiana Legislature visited the state penal farms at Angola and Hope for the purpose of reporting on the work done by the Board of Control, they spent considerable time in conversing with the negro convicts in order to elicit certain information.

One of the negroes chanced to recognize in a member of the committee a rising young member of the bar in New Orleans.

"It appears you know Mr. C——," remarked one of the committee.

"Yes, sah," responded the negro, grinning to show his teeth, "I knows him mighty well, sah; he wuz de genulman dat sent me heah."

"Is that so?" said the member who had addressed the darky. "I never knew that he had been a prosecuting attorney. How was it that he sent you here?"

"He was my lawyer, sah!" explained the convict.

Setting Himself Right

George Washington Thomas, an able-bodied negro of Sleepy Hollow, appeared before Magistrate Nussbaum charged with stealing chickens. The negro was accompanied by his lawyer, Colonel Simmons, a rising young white attorney. The old judge sauntered into the dingy court room, where he had reigned for more than twenty years, and, after calling for order, looked around on the little company there assembled. Seeing George Washington Thomas, he pointed to him and said:

"Are you the defendant in this case?"

Quick as a flash George was on his feet, and, not understanding legal terms, he exclaimed politely:

"No, sah; no, sah; I ain't de 'fen'ant; dar's de 'fen'ant ovah dar." And he pointed to his lawyer. There was a general laugh throughout the room, in which the old judge joined heartily. The darky felt abashed. He was visibly embarrassed, and, thinking to correct the mistake, if mistake it were, said again, pointing at his lawyer: "Yes, sah; he's de 'fen'ant," and pointing to himself, he said, "I's de genulman what stole de chickens."

CHAPTER XVI

The Irishman in Court

He Stood His Ground

A LEADING railroad lawyer, who has had much to do with human nature, says: "Never cross-question an Irishman from the old sod." And he gave an illustration from his own experience.

A section-hand had been killed by an express train and his widow was suing for damages. The main witness swore positively that the locomotive whistle had not sounded until after the whole train had passed over his departed friend.

"See here, McGinnis," said I, "you admit that the whistle blew?"

"Yis, sor, it blew, sor."

"Now, if that whistle sounded in time to give Michael warning, the fact would be in favor of the company, wouldn't it?"

"Yis, sor, and Mike would be tistifyin' here this day." The jury giggled.

"Very well. Now what earthly purpose could there be for the engineer to blow his whistle after Mike had been struck?"

"I preshume thot the whistle wor for the next man on the track, sor."

I quit, and the widow got all she asked.

What He Had Re(a)d

A story is going the rounds in a certain court house of an Irishman who recently went before Judge Stephens to be naturalized.

"Have you read the Declaration of Independence?" the judge asked.

"I hov not," said Pat.

"Have you read the Constitution of the United States?"

"I hov not, yer honor."

Judge Stephens looked sternly at the applicant and asked:

"Well, what have you read?"

Patrick hesitated but the fraction of a second before replying:

"I hov red hairs on me neck, yer honor."

Too Swift for Pat

The judge, lawyers, and everybody else were badgering an Irishman about the speed of a cart.

"Was it going fast?" queried the judge.

"Yis, it wor," answered the witness.

"How fast?"

"Oh, purty fasht, I guess it was, yer honor."

"Well, how fast?"

"Purty fasht."

"Was it going as fast as a man can run?"

"Aw, yis," said the Irishman, glad that a basis for an analogy was thus supplied him. "As fasht as two min kin run."

Got the Better of General Butler

During his boyhood Benjamin F. Butler was a frequent visitor in the town of Nottingham, New Hampshire, where his uncle, General Butler, resided. Among the many stories related of the general is one concerning his examination of Pat Murphy, a local character.

Tim Dolan had been accused of selling liquor, and the prosecution summoned Pat to testify in the case. Now Pat was a job teamster, and Butler endeavored to make him admit that he had delivered liquor to the defendant.

Butler asked: "Did you ever take any freight from the railroad office and deliver to Tim Dolan?"

"Yis, sor."

"Part of this freight was a barrel, wasn't it?"

"Yis, sor."

"Pat, what was in that barrel?"

"I don't know, sor!"

"Don't know! Wasn't the barrel marked?"

"Yis, sor."

"Then how dare you tell the court that you don't know what was in it?"

"Because, sor, the barrel was marked Tim Dolan on one end and bourbon whiskey on the other. How the divil did I know which was in it?"

Squelching a Witness

The Irish judge waxed wrathful at the long-winded replies of a facetious witness.

"I tell you what, my man," exclaimed his honor, "I won't listen to you any longer unless you can hold your tongue and give your evidence clearly."

In Defense of His Client

A young lawyer of Irish parentage, recently admitted to the New York bar, thus addressed the judge when about to begin the defense of his client in his first criminal case: "Your honor, I shall first absolutely prove to the jury that the prisoner could not have committed the crime with which he is charged. If that does not convince the jury, I shall show that he was insane when he committed it. If that fails, I shall prove an alibi."

Didn't Help His Case

Pat was ordinarily a good sort of citizen, but occasionally he would stray from the straight and narrow path, and during these diversions along the broader way where the water wagon rarely ran, he found enthusing ingredients that stirred his soul into strenuosity.

One day he became unusually ambitious and in the mêlée that followed one peacemaker went over the tree-tops and another just escaped having his name carved on a snow-white tombstone.

Consequently Pat got a personally conducted tour in a patrol wagon, and upon being taken into court was tried and convicted of attempting to deprive two worthy citizens of the right of franchise at all future elections.

"Prisoner at the bar, stand up," ordered the judge when the finding of the jury had been announced.

"All roight, yer honor," said Pat, assuming a perpendicular position.

"Prisoner at the bar," continued the judge, "have you anything to say why the sentence of the court should not be passed upon you?"

"No, yer honor," was the startling reply, "but it's mesilf that hopes yer hearrut will be as soft as yer head."

An Irish Repartee

Lawyer Dan O'Reilly was vigorously arguing a case in the West Side court in New York one day, when Magistrate Wahle interrupted him with the question:

"Is this Diogenes?"

The crowd on the bridge turned around and saw one of the prison keepers bearing a lighted lantern through the aisle.

"Yes, that is Diogenes," replied O'Reilly, "but he won't find the man he is looking for here."

A Personal Favor

One of the most picturesque figures of the New York bar was the late Thomas Nolan, a lawyer, whose witty retorts furnished subjects for merriment at many a lawyers' gathering. Now, Nolan was at one time counsel for a poor widow who was suing a construction company for the death of her husband. The case had been placed upon the "day calendar," but had been frequently postponed, and Mrs. Moriarty, by the time she had made her fifth call, was in an exceedingly disturbed frame of mind, consequently the tones of Nolan's rich brogue were more than usually fervid as he fought against the sixth adjournment.

"I am sorry," said Justice Dugro, "but your opponent has shown me good cause for the adjournment, Mr. Nolan, and the case will therefore go over until to-morrow."

"Very well, sor," said the barrister, sweetly, "but might I ask wan personal favor of this coort?"

"Certainly, sir, with pleasure."

"Will your honor kindly sthep down to my office and just tell Mrs. Moriarty that you have adjourned the case?"

As the Jury Decided

A barrister with a long experience of Irish juries in the mining regions of Pennsylvania, tells the following amusing story as illustrating their eccentricities.

A man was charged with committing a murderous assault upon another as a result of some political differences.

The assault having been committed at night, there appeared to be some difficulty in identifying the assailant, and, as a matter of fact, the counsel for the defense made out an excellent case for the prisoner, calling witnesses to testify that he was nowhere near the spot where the assault took place on the night in question.

Everybody concerned fully expected that the

jury would bring in a verdict of acquittal, yet, to the general astonishment, the foreman announced that the prisoner had been found guilty. "But," he added, observing the general consternation created by his statement, "not guilty of this assault, yer honor. This is the spalpeen who stole Biddy McCarthy's pig last year, and we foind him guilty of that!"

A Great Pity

Action was brought against a veterinary surgeon for causing the death of a man's horse. The judge, an Irishman by birth, knew something of medicine and asked if the dose given would not have killed the devil himself. The veterinary, drawing himself up pompously, said, "I never had the honor of attending that gentleman."

"That's a pity, doctor," replied the judge, "for he's alive still."

Can It Be?

Bridget was on the witness stand.

"You say," interposed the police justice, taking a hand in the investigation himself, "you heard the conversation between these two young men?"

"I did, yer honor," was the prompt reply.

"And it was just an ordinary conversation, such as two young men usually have when they meet?"

"Yis, yer honor."

"Yet you 'couldn't make head or tail' of what they were talking about?"

"No, yer honor."

"How was that?"

"Ivry other wur'rd was a cuss wur'rd, yer honor."

Might Have Been His Twin

"Were you present when the shot was fired?" asked the prosecuting attorney of the witness.

"Oi wuz, sor."

"Did you see who fired the shot?"

"Oi did."

"Who was it?"

"That mon, sor!" pointing to the prisoner.

"Are you sure of that?" from the counsel for the defense.

"Well, sor, if it wuzn't him, soir, it wuz afther bein' his twin brother."

CHAPTER XVII

The Young Lawyer

Why Return?

DESPITE the vast amount of legal business transacted in New York annually, there are so many lawyers there that the young man just starting his career has a very hard row to hoe. Lucky for him if he is well supplied with the world's goods, or if he has a few influential friends to give him a helping hand. Otherwise he is likely to have a bitter struggle with adversity before he lands squarely on his feet.

One young lawyer, who has a large and growing practice now, built up entirely through his own efforts, declares that more than once during the first few months after he was admitted to the bar he almost made up his mind to give up the fight and try some other line.

When he first started out, he hired an office in a down-town sky-scraper, and tried desperately hard to appear busy—much to the amusement of some of his neighbors, who saw through his "bluff." One day, on leaving his office, he placed a card on the door on which he had neatly written:

"Will return in an hour."

When he came back he found that some wag had added the words:

"For heaven's sake, why?"

Didn't Want a Lawyer

"I began to practice law in Dakota in Territorial days," said the lawyer from Chicago. "Our judges were sent to us, and some of them didn't know any more about law than they did about the political beliefs of the mound builders. One of them—I'll call him Jones—was so appallingly ignorant that it was a great relief when, on the admission of North Dakota to the Union, he left the bench and began to practice law. His successor was a man wholly without a sense of humor, and the only good thing he ever said in his life was wholly accidental. A man was brought to trial charged with selling liquor to the Indians. The judge asked him if he had a lawyer to defend him.

"'No,' said the man, 'I don't want a lawyer.'

"'Well,' said his honor, looking about the rooms till his eyes rested on his predecessor, 'I'll appoint Judge Jones to defend him.'"

Knew More Than the Lawyer

It was one of his first cases, and in a hesitating way he was questioning a witness as to the intelligence of a certain individual upon whose testimony hinged a very important point.

"Do you—do you consider Mr. Blank at all competent to form an—an opinion on this subject?"

"Yes, I guess he's somewhat so."

"How—how competent do you deem him to be?"

"Well, he doesn't know much about some things, but I guess all in all he knows a good sight more than you do."

His First Speech

A Virginia lawyer told this story:

"If a man can speak at all he certainly ought to do it well in a place like New York. There is everything there calculated to inspire, and loosen the tongue.

"It wasn't so when I was a young man in my state. I shall never forget the first time I was called out.

"I had just got my license to practice. The old ex-judge, in whose office I had read, was down to speak on the Fourth of July, at a picnic in the woods. At the last minute he had to send word that he could not be present.

"He sent me on horseback to the woods to inform the committee. I traveled at a Paul Revere gait. When I reached the platform the people were waiting, and the committee in their sashes and regalia were on the stand.

"As soon as I had orally delivered the judge's message of regret the chairman proclaimed it to the multitude and announced that as the judge couldn't come his young law student—meaning me—would take his place.

"I explained to the chairman and the committee that I had never made a speech, and that I certainly would not attempt to make one on that occasion. The more I protested the more the committee insisted.

"During the wrangle on the stand the people began to howl for Judge ——'s young man to pitch in. The committee got behind me and pushed me to the improvised rail.

"Just at that moment Providence came to my rescue. Somebody yelled 'Fire!' The next minute a young man as tall and thin as a sapling leaped about six feet in the air and screamed like a scared Indian.

"He wore a long linen duster. As he leaped, the tail of his coat flashed up in flame and smoke and he made a bee-line for a creek near by. The crowd followed. The committee leaped over the rail and joined in the pursuit. The chairman yelled at every jump, 'Put him out! put him out!'

"The fellow had just lighted his pipe as I was pushed to the rail and in dropping the burning match it fell into his pocket and started the conflagration. While the crowd followed him to the creek I leaped from the platform, mounted my horse, and rode away. By the time the chap reached the water I was out of sight.

"I have made many speeches since that time, but I never got on my feet that the recollection of my first escape from an audience did not come before me. My old law preceptor used to say of me that I was a born orator, and I moved my first audience without uttering a single word."

Might Repeal All He Knew

Some time before the late George Vest became a Senator of the United States he was one of a commission which was examining applicants for admission to the Missouri bar. A youthful aspirant had failed in several branches of the examination.

"I regret to say," remarked Mr. Vest, "that you have failed to come up to the mark in the branches of law upon which we have examined you. But," he added in a most kindly spirit, "we will question you further if you desire."

"Well, sir," responded the aspirant, "I would suggest, if you please, that I be questioned on the statutes."

At this Mr. Vest smiled sadly. "My dear young man," added he, "I do not doubt that you're up on the statutes; but I do doubt that you will succeed in the law. Suppose you should have the utmost familiarity with the statutes, what's to prevent the Legislature from repealing all you know?"

Difficult to Believe

Jennings is a young lawyer who some time ago established his home in a suburb where a cot, with an acre of ground and a cow, is supposed to be the earthly paradise. His chum, Brown, also of the bar, after hearing of the rural delights for a long time, consented finally to spend a Sunday on "the farm." He was received with all the honors and all the attractions were shown to him.

At each meal he had to listen to eulogies of "our own make" viands. He stood patiently our own milk, lettuce from that frame you saw, peas off the vine in the back lot, and so on until it got to "Harry, I can recommend this chicken specially. I raised it myself."

Then the worm turned with a sad smile and remarked:

"No, Will, I can't believe that. You've only been here a little over two years!"

Depew's Subtle Argument

One of the first cases which Chauncey Depew had after being admitted to the bar was a civil suit involving a somewhat complicated question of inheritance.

In no way daunted, young Chauncey tackled it, looked up authorities all the way back to Julius Cæsar, and prepared an argument of a few hundred pages which seemed to him more than unanswerable. His only fear was that it might be beyond the comprehension of the court.

When the time came the young man rose and plunged in boldly. The judge seemed interested, and Chauncey took further courage. But at the end of an hour and a half, in the midst of the most intricate part of his plea, he was pained to see what he thought was a lack of attention on the part of the court. It was just as he had expected: the judge was unable to appreciate the nice points of his argument.

He paused, hesitated, and then said: "Your honor, I beg pardon, but do you follow me?"

"I have so far," answered the judge, shifting about in his chair; "but I'll say frankly that if I thought I could find my way back I'd quit right here."

He Couldn't Do It

"Say, pop," inquired the youngster who had accompanied his father to court, as he pointed to a recently admitted attorney conducting his first case, "who is that fellow that tries to talk like the lawyers?"

Wisdom That Comes With Age

I well remember one case before a justice in which I acted as respondent's counsel in a criminal action and in which an older and well-known attorney was my opponent. As I thought then, and as I know now, the law and the evidence were well in favor of my client, and at the close of the arguments I looked with great confidence for a prompt acquittal. Judge of my astonishment when my unfortunate client was found guilty and sentenced to thirty days in jail. I promptly entered an appeal, and furnished sureties to prosecute the same. Before I left the court room the justice took occasion to take me aside and say: "Young man, I kinder thought ye were right, but I know Judge W—— (naming my opponent) is a sight older'n you be, and a sight better lawyer'n you be, and so of course I gave him judgment."

A Quick Trial

The following is an account of one of the shortest criminal trials on record:

The jury having been impaneled and the prisoner arraigned, the witness for the prosecution steps into the box, and, before he has had time to look around to see where the voice comes from, he is thus examined by the prosecuting counsel:

"I think you were walking up Fifth Street on Wednesday, June 16th, about ten o'clock in the evening, and suddenly felt a pull at your coat pocket and missed your wallet, containing $350.00, which the constable now produces. Is that it?"

"Yes, sir."

"I suppose you have nothing to ask him?" says the judge to the counsel for the defense. "Next witness."

Constable stands up.

"Were you following the prosecutor on the occasion when he was robbed on Fifth Street, and did you see the prisoner put his hand into the prosecutor's pocket and take this wallet out of it?"

"Yes, sir."

Judge to prisoner: "Nothing to say, I suppose?" Then to the jury: "Gentlemen, I suppose you have no doubt? I have none."

Jury: "Guilty, your honor."

Judge to prisoner: "Jenkins, we have met before—we shall not meet again for some time—three years in the penitentiary—next case."

Time: two minutes, fifty-three seconds.

The young lawyer who was to have conducted the defense was so dumbfounded that he could not utter a word.

Crux vs. Crooks

The young attorney was making his first argument before the Supreme Court and was impressed with the importance of the event. The two witnesses for the other side were an ex-convict and a private detective.

"The crux of this whole case, your honor," he began.

The two witnesses looked insulted, the judge

smiled, and the lawyer for the other side was on his feet in a minute.

"Crooks?" he repeated. "May I ask the learned counsel for the defense whether he is speaking Latin or English?"

"Latin," he replied, and it was not until the argument was over that he understood why the court was so amused and the opposing attorney so indignant.

CHAPTER XVIII

Coroners' Verdicts

Coroners' Verdicts

SOME of the country coroners' verdicts of fifty and sixty years ago are very curious. The following are some of the causes assigned for death:

"She come to her death by strangulation in testimony we have sit our hands and seal the day above wroten."

"Paul Burns came to his death by a mule running away with a wagon and being thrown therefrom."

"By taking with his own hands an overdose of morphine."

"From causes unknown to the jury and having no medical attendance."

"Came to his death from national causes."

"An inquisition holden upon the body of John Brown there lying dead by the jurors whose names are hereto subscribed, who upon oath do say that he came to his death in the following manner, by falling off the plank bridge accidental while trying to cross the stream and was drowned."

"Said child, aged one day old, came to her death from spasms, said child having been found by the witness in a trunk, under very suspicious circumstances."

"The joueres on thare ouathe do say that he come to his deth by old age, as tha could not see ennything else the matter."

"Come to his death from the following causes, to wit: from some suddent cause to the juoeres unknown."

"The said deceased being an orphan, father and mother being both dead."

"From an overdose of gin administered by his own hand."

"Disability caused by lunacy."

"Said infant child came to his death from premature birth."

"Death by canser of the gravel."

"Being run over by two coal trucks, while detached from the engine."

"Come to his death by tender No. 7 jumping the track, on which he was riding, either jumping or falling off and engine running over him, which was an accident and no fault of the engineer of said engine."

"She come to her death by the lighten striken her."

"From hart deseize."

"Come to his death in the following manner to wit: He was born dead."

"From excessive drinking and laying out in the sun."

"From the hands of some person or persons to the jury unknown and afterward placed on the track and got run over by incoming train."

"Congestion of the brain an applicote fitze."

"The body was so mangled and mutilate that tha could not tell ennything about it, but tha think it was put in the sisterne by some unknown person or persons."

"Diseas of the hart and applexity fitze."

"Calded on the left side by kittley of hot water burning over on hir left side and immegitely causing her death."

"From the effect of injuries received by her close accidental taking fire."

"From exposier."